How to Specify Yo...

A methodical approach to all the decisions for buying or building the right bicycle

Dave Peart

About this Book

Whether you are seeking guidance for buying a complete new bike, upgrading your current one or looking to build one from individual components, this book walks you through the process from start to finish – ensuring you are clear on your needs and that the end-result delivers accordingly.

This book will also help you determine the correct type of bike as well as understand all the features you need to consider, such as the type of brakes, gear-ratio selection and the different component standards available.

Key considerations and trade-offs such as cost and weight are described in detail, with worked examples provided to help you with budgeting.

Guidelines are also provided regarding where to buy your bike and components as well as useful information of what to be aware of when assembling your components. The book is not however a workshop manual and thus does not provide build instructions – a subject probably better served by the wealth of material on YouTube!

The scope of this book includes road bikes, mountain bikes, gravel bikes and hybrid bikes. The general principles included in the book will also apply to other types of bikes but specific information is not included for children's bikes, BMX or e-bikes.

Disclaimer

This guide is not intended for the treatment or prevention of disease, nor as a substitute for medical treatment, nor as an alternative to medical advice. It is presented for information purposes only. Use of this guide is at the sole choice and risk of the reader. The author shall remain free of any fault, liability or responsibility for any loss or harm, whether real or perceived, resulting from the use of information in this guide.

The information provided within this guide is understood to be correct at the time of writing, the author cannot be held responsible for omissions, errors or subsequent changes. No guarantee is provided for function or compatibility of the components you choose to use.

Acknowledgements

This book would not have been possible to research nor have much practical value without the wide selection of highly competitive internet retailers such as Chain Reaction Cycles, Wiggle, Planet X, Ribble Cycles, Merlin Cycles, Tredz and many more.

I would also like to thank James Ryan from Boardman Bikes, Simon Whiten from Handsling Bikes and Planet X for their kind provision of images of the bikes included within this book.

Contents

Follow the process

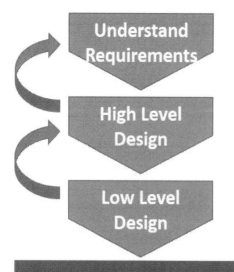

Understand Requirements
- Be clear about what you need
- Identify your budget

High Level Design
- Determine key features
- Set target cost & weight

Low Level Design
- Make sure everything will work
- Confirm cost & weight

Complete Specification

Procure
- Select where to buy & place order

Build & Tune
- Assemble the bike
- Adjust/amend

1. Introduction

Walking You through the Process

This book follows a logical process (as illustrated in the diagram on the adjacent page), which starts by helping you to understand your requirements before going through iterative loops of high level and low level design to arrive at the complete specification, which can then be used for ordering and building your bike.

Jargon

The world of bikes and cycling is full of jargon that can put-off and confuse both beginners and experienced riders from buying a bike or making changes to their existing bikes. To help you start the process of specifying your bike, some of the most frequent terms are explained below.

Term	Meaning
Alloy	Usually an abbreviation for alloys of Aluminium - covered in more detail later in the book.
Carbon	An abbreviation of Carbon Fibre (also termed "carbon fibre reinforced plastic/polymer" or "carbon composite") – covered in more detail later in the book.
Clipless Shoes/Pedals	A system that enables shoes to attach securely to the pedals but which also releases with a sideways twist – similar to ski bindings.
Derailleur(s)	The mechanism(s) that move the chain between the different sprockets (either the front sprockets on the chainset, or rear sprockets on cassette on the rear wheel) to change the gear ratio.
Direct-mount	A term used for a multitude of components such as brakes and derailleurs – take care if this term is mentioned and read the relevant sections in the Low Level Design chapter.
Disc Brakes	Brakes which function with a caliper that pushes brake pads against a disc rotor mounted to the centre of the wheel.
Drop Handlebars	Shape of handlebar typically used on road (racing) bikes with a "curly" shape, which has a number of options for hand positions and enables a more aerodynamic riding position than with straight handlebars.
Dropper seatpost	A method of raising or lowering the saddle with a button/lever without having to stop to get off the bike.
Full Suspension	A bike that has suspension mechanisms for both the front and rear wheels.
Gear Ratio	The speed the wheels rotate relative to the crank/pedals (a higher ratio means the wheels rotate faster and therefore require more force to be applied to the pedals).
Groupset	A collective term for all the gear and brake components on a bike.
Hardtail	A bike with front suspension only (i.e. no suspension for the rear wheel).
Mech	Abbreviation for "mechanism" - another term for derailleur.
Rim Brakes	Brakes which function with a caliper that pushes brake pads against the wheel rims.
Shifters	Levers that are used to change gear.
Sportive	A long-distance organised cycling event typically ridden on a road bike.
Sprocket	The toothed wheel (cog) that engages with the chain.
Tubeless	Tyres that seal air-tight to the rim without an innertube (similar to a car tyre).

Be clear about what you need

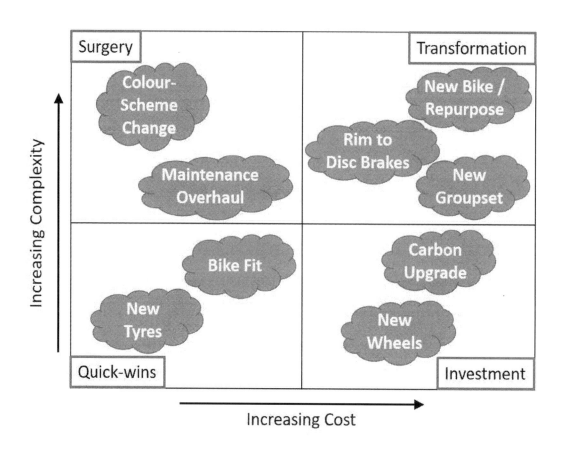

2. Understanding Your Requirements

Scoping your Project

The first thing to establish is the scale of the project you have in mind, both in terms of cost and complexity. The adjacent diagram highlights a range of typical projects, categorised as follows:

- Quick wins – these are low-cost and easy-to-fit changes that will make a noticeable difference to the bike, such as upgrading the tyres or undergoing a bike fit (which might require changes to handlebars, stem or saddle).

- Investments – these are higher cost yet easy-to-fit changes such as a new set of wheels or changing various alloy components to carbon fibre (e.g. stem, seatpost and/or even wheels).

- Surgery – this category of upgrades are relatively low-cost but will be fairly complex to install, such as changing all the colour-coordinated components (e.g. cables, bar tape/grips) or giving the bike a maintenance overhaul and replacing worn components.

- Transformation – these involve both high costs and mechanically complex changes, such as swapping the entire groupset, converting from rim to disc brakes or a complete bike build/repurpose project (e.g. converting an older bike into a winter bike).

Partial Upgrade or Whole Bike

This book covers all the components that constitute a bike, both in terms of the context of components to the rest of the bike, and the specific details of individual components.

There are two approaches you can take to reading this book:

1) If you are planning a whole-bike project, such as a complete new bike or the re-purpose / major upgrade of an existing one, then I would recommend that you follow the book from start to finish as this will guide you through the decision making processes in the intended sequence.

2) If you are planning a partial upgrade and are reasonably clear on the scope, then start with the relevant section of the High Level Design chapter and then jump to the relevant sections of Low Level Design. (You may also wish to read the book from start to finish or just jump in as and when you decide to upgrade or replace components.)

Road Bike Top Five Upgrades

If you have a mainstream road bike, these are the component upgrades likely to make the most difference: (but read the relevant sections of the book to determine your needs)

1) Saddle – you might be lucky and not have any issues from your saddle, but a incorrectly fitting saddle could lead to extreme discomfort and put you off riding for life – worth a trip to a bike shop with saddle-fitting facilities;
2) Bike Fit – see a reputable bike-fitter to get the saddle, cleats and handlebars in the optimum positions, as this will have a major impact on comfort and cycling efficiency;
3) Cassette – if you ride hills, then go wide-ratio; if you stay flat, then go close-range (probably wise to also change your chain at the same time - also check the compatibility of the rear mech);
4) Tyres and tubes – a relatively low-cost way to optimise the balance between lower weight, less rolling resistance, puncture resistance, more grip or more comfort;
5) Wheels (e.g. entry-level to high-spec alloy, or alloy to carbon, or shallow to deep section).

MTB Top Five Upgrades

If you have a mainstream mountain bike, these are the component upgrades likely to make the most difference (but read the relevant sections of the book to determine your needs):

1) Bike Fit – this is more likely to be DIY (but you may find a MTB-specific fitter), key checks are handlebar width and height, stem length, saddle position and suspension adjustments;
2) Tubeless Tyres – (assuming your rims cooperate) this change will allow you to use lower pressures to give more grip, whilst also improving puncture protection and reducing weight;
3) Dropper seatpost – to allow you control over saddle height without stopping;
4) Suspension – an expensive upgrade, but upgrading the forks and/or rear shock will have a major impact on the bike's handling.
5) Wheels – optimised for weight, width and strength to suit your style of riding;

Whole Bike Requirements

What kind of bike...

If you are in the market for a new bike (or the re-purpose of an existing bike), it is essential to choose the type of bike that best meets your needs. This may result in balancing a number of factors if you want a single bike, or it may be that you follow the path of multiple bikes for different types of riding.

Follow the flow chart below as a start-point to select the relevant genre of bike.

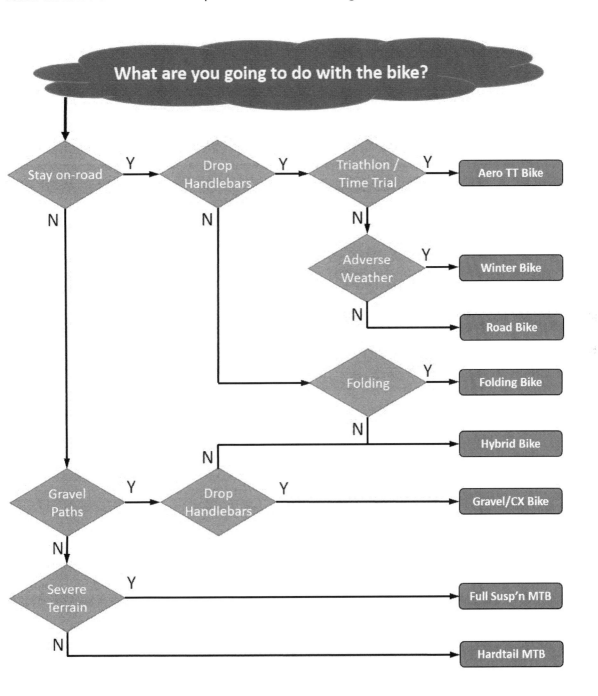

One Bike or Two (or more…)

According to the "rules of cycling" (http://www.velominati.com/the-rules/), Rule 12 states that the correct number of bikes own is n+1 (where n = the number of bikes you currently own). Thus is the predicament of choosing a general bike (and having fewer bikes) or a more specific bike for the function in mind (and having more).

If you have conflicting needs of your bike (e.g. want to ride rough terrain but also want to be able to ride long distances on the road) then the answer may be to divide your budget between two bikes – or choose the more urgent need initially with a view of procuring another genre of bike at a later date. Note also the risk of compromising in the middle, with for example a single hybrid bike, you may struggle to keep up with others riding road bikes and also suffer with terrain other than basic gravel paths.

Bike Genres & Key Differences

The following table lists out the key features & differences between the major genres of road bikes, and the following pages provide a more detailed profile on each one. Review these carefully and objectively to confirm which bike you intend to specify.

Genre	Key Features	Good For…	Not Good For…
Summer Road Bike	Narrow tyres, Light-weight	Riding at a fast pace on roads and smooth cycle paths	Off-road riding, Typically without sufficient frame/fork clearance for wider tyres
Winter Road Bike	Wider tyres with tread, Mudguards, Ideally with disc brakes	Riding on roads in wet/wintery conditions	Typically heavier and lower-spec than a Summer Bike
Aero/TT	Aerodynamic components (e.g. aero bars), Low & forward riding position	Triathlons, Time-trial racing	General riding, Wet or wintery weather
Gravel/ Cyclo-cross (CX)	Similar to a Winter Bike but with wider tyres to cope with off-road riding Typically with disc brakes	Riding on bridlepaths and non-technical single-track paths, Competing in CX events, Can also be used as a Winter Bike	Slightly slower than road bike Not as capable off-road as a MTB
Hybrid	Flat handlebars Typically without suspension	Very versatile bike, can tailor spec significantly	Not as fast-pace as road bike Not as capable off-road as MTB
Folding	Able to fold for commuting, transport or storage	Commuting on trains, transporting in car boot	Longer distance, faster pace riding or off-road use
Full-Suspension MTB	Front & rear suspension Wide tyres Wide range of gears Powerful disc brakes	Off-road riding, especially with rocks & jumps	Distance-riding on roads Heavier than Hardtail MTB
Hardtail MTB	Front suspension only Wide tyres Wide range of gears Powerful disc brakes	Off-road riding on trails	Fast-pace road-riding Extreme terrain

Summer Road Bike

Purpose: To enable you to ride on roads as efficiently and as comfortably as possible (in fair weather).

Why choose this bike: If you intend to ride on the roads in fair weather conditions.

When not to choose this bike: Not ideal (but many people do use) for wet-weather and winter riding. Not ideal for off-road use.

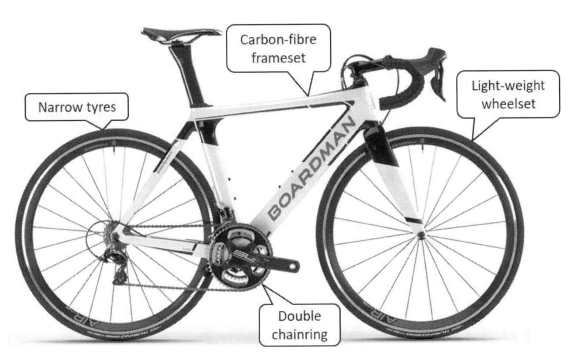

Key Features:

- Low bike weight (relative to budget) with components such as a carbon-fibre frameset and lightweight wheels and tyres.
- Narrow tyres (e.g. 25mm);
- Frame geometry with shallower angles for a more comfortable and less-twitchy ride;
- Double chainring with 10, 11 or 12 sprockets on the rear cassette (giving a total of 20-24 gears).

Main Specification Decisions:

- If this is to be your primary bike, then consider tyre clearance for mudguards and wider tyres for winter use. If this is to be your prized fair-weather bike then you can focus more on exotic materials and lower weight;
- Budget - which will govern the choice of materials and specification of wheels and groupset;
- Gear ratios - depending on your local terrain;
- Brake specification: rim vs. disc, cable vs. hydraulic (the trend is growing towards disc brakes, even for fair-weather road bikes).

Winter Road Bike

Purpose: To enable you to ride on roads as comfortably as possible during wet and/or wintery weather conditions - typically a lower-cost bike to save your more expensive prized bike for fair weather riding.

Why choose this bike: If you intend to ride on the roads in all weather conditions - potentially having this as a second bike of lesser value than your prized bike. This type of bike would also make a good touring bike.

When not to choose this bike: A winter bike is very versatile and can also be used through the summer. The main reasons for not choosing a winter bike could be if you want to spend all your money on a lighter-weight or aerodynamic bike, or plan to ride off-road - in which case choose a Gravel Bike.

Key Features:

- Sufficient tyre-clearance for both frame and forks to fit wider tyres and mudguards;
- Wider tyres (e.g. 25-30mm) - also consider going tubeless;
- Frame geometry with shallower angles for a more comfortable and less-twitchy ride;
- Consider choosing disc brakes for better braking when wet and to avoid wearing-out wheel rims.

Main Specification Decisions:

- If this is to be your primary bike, then use your budget wisely. If this is a second bike, then choose durability over weight-saving;
- Gear ratios - depending on your local terrain;
- Brake specification: rim vs. disc, cable vs. hydraulic;
- Tyre width, tread and puncture resistance;

Mounting points for racks etc. if you are planning to use the bike for touring.

Aero / Time-trail Bike

Purpose: To achieve the most optimal aerodynamic profile (and pedalling position) for rider and bike.

Why choose this bike: If you intend to compete in time trials or triathlons or have specific riding/training objectives that will benefit significantly from improved aerodynamics.

When not to choose this bike: For general, sportive or social riding on hilly terrain or any form of off-road use; also not ideal in wet or wintery weather conditions.

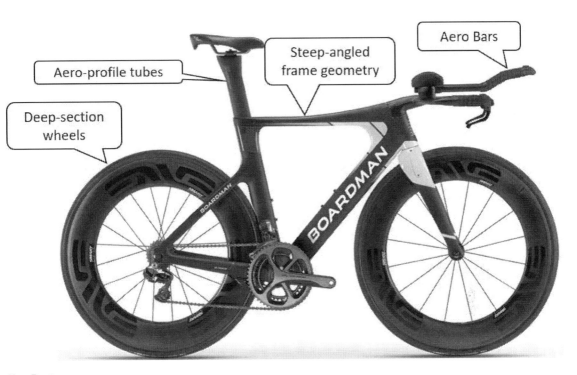

Key Features:

- Frame geometry with steeper angles to enable a more aerodynamic riding position;
- Aero bars for a more aerodynamic riding position. Note: this may be base-bars with extensions (as per picture above) or drop handlebars with extensions or an integrated one-piece unit;
- Deeper-section wheels (less drag);
- Aerodynamically-profiled frame and fork tubes (and seatpost in the above picture).

Main Specification Decisions:

- Budget - which will govern the choice of materials and specification of wheels and groupset;
- Gear ratios;
- Handlebar configuration (base bar or drop-handlebars with extensions).

Gravel / Adventure / Cyclocross Bike

Purpose: A drop-handlebar bike that can be ridden efficiently on the road as well as taken off-road on gravel tracks and bridleways.

Why choose this bike: If you want to cover longer distances (higher on-road speeds) than a mountain bike but also want the flexibility to ride on off-road paths and tracks. If fitted with mudguards, then this type of bike will double as a winter bike. This type of bike would also be well-suited for cyclocross riding.

When not to choose this bike: If you want the ultimate on-road performance (i.e. choose a road bike) or want to ride more technical off-road tracks (i.e. choose a mountain bike).

Note: Cyclo-cross Bikes (for CX racing) need to comply with racing regulations, whereas with general Gravel Bikes you have complete freedom on your specification.

Wider tyres

Wide range gears

Disc Brakes

Key Features:

- Mid-size tyres (e.g. 30-40mm) - often tubeless for greater puncture resilience;
- Wide range of gears - often with a single (1x) chainring;
- Typically fitted with disc brakes;
- Sufficient clearance for mudguards.

Main Specification Decisions:

- Budget - which will govern the choice of materials and specification of wheels and groupset;
- Tyre width and specification (e.g. tubeless, which will drive the wheel specification);
- Gear ratios and configuration - study the Low Level Design chapter carefully;
- Brake specification: rim vs. disc, cable vs. hydraulic.

Hybrid Bike

Purpose: A general purpose affordable bike.

Why choose this bike: If you want an affordable bike without drop handlebars that can be used on-road and for off-road gravel tracks and paths.

When not to choose this bike: If you want to ride at faster speeds (in which case choose a road bike) or want to ride on more severe off-road terrain (in which case choose a mountain bike).

Key Features:

- Flat handlebars, typically around 600mm wide (narrower than MTB handlebars);
- Mid-size tyres (e.g. 30-40mm);
- Wide range of gears to suit most terrains;
- Mounting points on the frame and forks for mudguards and racks.

Main Specification Decisions:

- Whether you need front suspension or not (adds cost & weight);
- Tyre width - if you have any specific needs (e.g. narrow for mainly road use, or wider and knobbly if more off-road)
- Gear ratios - depending on your local terrain;
- Brake specification: rim vs. disc, cable vs. hydraulic;
- Mounting points for racks etc. if you are planning to use the bike for touring.

Folding Bike

Purpose: To enable you to collapse the bike sufficiently to fit your needs (e.g. take on trains, fit in car, etc.)

Why choose this bike: If being able to fold the bike is of primary importance.

When not to choose this bike: If you can come up with other solutions allowing you to use a regular bike.

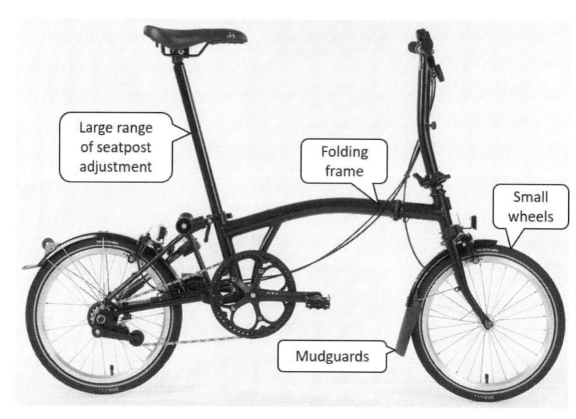

Key Features:

- Ability to fold (e.g. hinges in frame, stem and chain-stays)
- Small wheels (e.g. 16-20 inch);
- Large range of adjustment for seatpost;
- Mudguards - essential for commuting.

Main Specification Decisions:

- Size of folded bike - will determine if you can fit in luggage rack on a train or in your car boot;
- Budget - Brompton bikes are not cheap (but are very good and do fold compactly)!
- Bike weight vs. features - consider how much carrying of the bike you are likely to do (e.g. up and down train station steps);
- Gear ratios;
- Features such as mudguards, racks, lights, etc.

Hardtail Mountain Bike

Purpose: A lighter-weight, more affordable and nimble mountain bike - but more resilient than a hybrid bike.

Why choose this bike: If you want to ride off-road trails without tackling the more technical features.

When not to choose this bike: If you want to tackle the more technically-demanding trails and can justify the need and budget for a full-suspension bike; or if a hybrid bike will meet your needs.

Key Features:

- Front suspension only, typically with 100-140mm travel;
- Lighter-weight MTB-specific tyres (e.g. 50+mm) - typically tubeless for greater puncture resilience;
- Wide range of gears - often with a single (1x) chainring (but not always - as per above picture)
- Hydraulic disc brakes;

Main Specification Decisions:

- Budget - which will govern the choice of materials and specification of fork, wheels and groupset;
- General - lighter weight where possible without weakening the bike;
- Tyre/wheel diameter, width and specification;
- Gear ratios and configuration;
- Fixed or dropper seatpost;
- Flat pedals or clipless;

Full-suspension Mountain Bike (Enduro / All Mountain)

Purpose: For riding down technical trails and typically riding back up to the top.

Why choose this bike: If you want to ride demanding technical trails, whereby you will appreciate the benefits of rear suspension over a hardtail, and where you expect to ride back up to the top (rather than rely on a shuttle service).

When not to choose this bike: If you don't need rear suspension (i.e. choose a hardtail) or if you intend to ride more extreme downhill trails (i.e. choose a downhill bike).

Key Features:

- Front and rear suspension, typically with 130-170mm travel;
- Wider tyres (e.g. 2.1-2.4") - typically tubeless for greater puncture resilience and lower pressures;
- Wide range of gears - typically with a single (1x) chainring;
- Hydraulic disc brakes (e.g. 180mm rotors);

Main Specification Decisions:

- Budget - which will govern the choice of materials and specification of suspension, wheels and groupset;
- General - a balance of strength/durability and weight;
- Tyre/wheel diameter, width and specification;
- Gear ratios and configuration;
- Fixed or dropper seatpost;
- Flat pedals or clipless;

Full-suspension Mountain Bike (Downhill)

Purpose: For riding down the most extreme trails and typically getting a shuttle service back up to the top.

Why choose this bike: If you want to ride down the toughest trails, requiring more suspension travel and strength than an enduro-style bike - and where you expect a shuttle service (or to push) up to the top.

When not to choose this bike: If you don't plan to ride extreme trails or if you expect any notable pedalling uphill.

Key Features:

- 200mm suspension travel front and rear - typically with dual-crown forks;
- Slack head angle (e.g. 63°);
- Limited range of gears - typically single (1x) chainring with a 7-speed cassette;
- Chain retention features;
- Hydraulic disc brakes with 203mm rotors and four-piston calipers.

Main Specification Decisions:

- Budget - which will govern the choice of materials and specification of suspension, wheels and groupset;
- General - strength and durability rather than lower weight;
- Tyre/wheel diameter, width and specification;
- Gear ratios and configuration;
- Flat pedals or clipless;

Buy Whole or Build It Yourself?

This will be a very personal decision, depending on your situation. Please bear in mind the following when making this decision:

- Do you have the skills & tools required to build your own bike (or an amenable local bike shop)?
- Do you want the fall-back of a guarantee or a "change of mind" policy?
- Have you considered using a Cycle-to-Work scheme to fund a complete bike?

Generally you get 20-30% more for your money when buying a complete bike as you will benefit from the manufacturers buying power and economies of scale. However you may find that none of the bikes off-the-shelf give you all the component specifications that you want. Other more specific factors to consider are:

- Is there a whole bike that offers most of what you want that you can upgrade later?
- Are any of the major components on offer with significant discounts (e.g. end-of-season sale)?
- Do you have spare components from previous bikes that you could re-use to keep the cost down?
- Are you seeking the challenge of building a bike...

If after reading this chapter you are still undecided whether to buy whole or build, then continue reading to the end of the book before you make up your mind!

Budget Setting and Future Upgrades

At this stage, it is vital to set a budget and also to have a view on whether you would plan any upgrades to the bike in the future. For example, a new set of wheels is an easy-to-fit upgrade that could make a noticeable difference to the feel of the bike, however you may need to spend a significant amount of money for such a change; deferring would save you the initial outlay and allow you more time to save, choose or wait for the sales.

There are other potential upgrades which are not so easy, such as changing from 10-speed to 11-speed (detailed explanations to follow later in the book) that are better to embrace from the start.

Cascading Upgrades Down through Your Fleet

Another consideration at this stage (that might help with your budget planning and investment justification!) is whether there is feasibility to cascade replaced components onto other bikes you may own.

As an example, the table below shows a scenario of owning three bikes, whereby:

- The Best Bike retains its original frameset but had new wheels two years ago; new bars, stem and seat last year; and a new groupset this year.
- Bike 2 still has its original frameset, it has the other components off the Best Bike and has just had a new set of wheels.
- Bike 3 has inherited all the replaced parts from above that still have useful life left in them.

	Frameset	Groupset	Wheels	Finishing Kit
Best Bike		New	2 Years	Last Year
Bike 2			New	
Bike 3				
Spare/Scrap				

But before you spend any time thinking about how the above might work for you, it is essential that you consider the genres of bike that you will use and the specific requirements of each of them - otherwise you may just end up with three summer bikes, instead of potentially a summer bike, a properly specified winter bike and a capable TT bike!

Requirements Statement

Before proceeding with the rest of the book, please write down your answers for the following questions (do this for each bike if you are planning more than one):

1) Which type of bike best meets your needs?
2) What is the maximum budget you can afford?
3) What is your current thinking regarding buying a whole bike or building one yourself?
4) Are there any upgrades you could defer to the future?

Determine key features

Requirements Statement

Tyres & Wheels

Brakes

Gears

Frame & Forks

High Level Specification

3. High Level Design

This chapter will take you through the considerations of the major components that define a bike and prompt you to make decisions that will steer the general specification of the bike to align with your needs.

Pitching the bike at the right level

As Keith Bontrager once said: "strong, light, cheap – pick two"!

- If you want a bike that is both strong and lightweight, then expect to pay more!
- If funds are limited, then strong components will be heavy and light components may break or wear quickly!

… so begins the iterative process of choosing what you want, adding up the total cost & weight, and then going back around and around the loop until you've optimised appropriately and concluded your specification.

Time spent agonising over details at this stage is well spent considering the potential amount of time that you will spend riding the bike over future years (and the money you'll spend)!

Major Component Groups

The High Level Design phase of the process focuses on specification decisions rather than product choices (e.g. wheel/tyre size & material rather than make/model). The process of decision making follows on from the Requirements Statement and covers the major component groups as illustrated in the adjacent diagram.

The aim of this stage of the process is to define the bike with respect to its key features and set both the target cost and weight. The aim is also to achieve this High Level Specification through as few decisions as necessary.

The major component groups and the rationale for including them for the High Level Design are:

Tyres and Wheels	Fundamentally determines the size and usage of the bike and significantly narrows-down the choice of frame and forks.
Brakes	The choice of brake-type constrains the frame/forks options as well as the choice of wheels.
Gears	Decisions such as gear-type, ratio-range and number of chainrings are fundamental to the definition of the bike, and also constrain many other specification decisions.
Frame and Forks	After taking all of the above into account, the frame and forks define the ride and handling of the bike as well as the aesthetics.

Tyres & Wheels

The most significant component group, which drives the specification choices for the rest of the bike, is the tyres and wheels. The key decisions to address are shown in the following diagram.

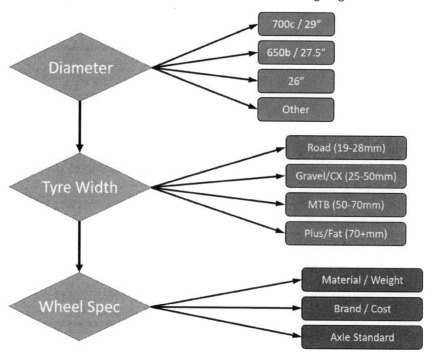

Tyre/Wheel Diameter

This is a very confusing subject of interchangeable metric and imperial units with measurements taken across different aspects of wheels and tyres. The following table should help clarify this subject, the mainstream sizes are highlighted – but be careful if upgrading an existing bike or re-using components!

Description	ETRTO Dimension	Notes
700c	622mm	Most road bikes use this diameter of wheel/tyre (occasionally referred to as 28") – widths usually quoted in mm
29"	622mm	This is the same size as the above, but is more commonly used to describe mountain bikes – widths usually quoted in inches
650b / 27.5"	584mm	Typically found on mountain bikes, generally considered lighter and more manoeuvrable than 29" wheels – widths quoted in inches
27"	630mm	Not typically found today other than on vintage road bikes
650c	571mm	Niche size, not in mainstream use
26"	559mm	Common standard of wheel/tyre for mountain bikes and hybrid bikes – widths usually quoted in inches
24"	540mm	Older size of wheel for smaller-wheeled racing bikes
24"	520mm	Older size of wheel for 24" BMX bikes
24"	507mm	Typically found on children's mountain-style bikes with wider tyres
20"	406mm	Mainstream BMX size and used for children's bikes
16"	349mm	Used on Brompton folding bikes

Note: ETRTO refers to the European Tyre and Rim Technical Organisation and the size refers to the diameter of the wheel where the tyre bead seats.

Tyre Width

The width and the inflation pressure of the tyres will determine the ride and handling performance of the bike. Narrow slick tyres at high pressures will roll fast but with very little compliance over bumps and virtually zero traction in muddy conditions, whereas wide knobbly tyres at lower pressures will offer fantastic grip, absorb the bumps but with an overhead of higher rolling resistance.

The table below outlines the mainstream spectrum of tyre choice.

Width	Usage	Notes
19-28mm	Road bikes and hybrid bikes for mainly road use	Most common widths for road bikes are: 23mm – with tyre pressures of 100+psi 25mm – can be used at slightly lower pressures (90 psi) 28mm – much more comfortable to ride, but heavier and will limit the choice of frameset due to required tyre clearance. Tyres in this category typically have minimal tread pattern, but some winter-style tyres will offer slightly more tread. Most common diameter is 700c (622mm). Limited selection of tubeless tyres (but growing)
25-50mm (1" – 2")	Gravel, cyclocross and hybrid bikes for off-road paths as well as road use	Available in a variety of tread patterns to suit the intended balance of road/off-road usage. This category of tyres typically run much lower pressures than road bikes (e.g. 40-70 psi) and are much more forgiving over bumpy surfaces. Most common diameter is 700c (622mm) when width is listed in mm. Most common diameter is 26" (559mm) when width is listed in inches. Limited selection of tubeless tyres.
50-70mm (2" – 2.75")	Mountain bikes and hybrid bikes used more off-road than on-road	Extensive variety of tread patterns available, tyre pressures typically 30-50 psi. Widely available across 29" (622mm), 650b/27.5" (584mm) and 26" (559mm) – width usually listed in inches Wide selection of tubeless tyres.
70+mm (>2.8")	Plus / Fat bikes	Extra wide tyres for use on Plus and Fat bikes, can run very low pressures (e.g. <20 psi). Typically used tubeless on 650b/27.5" (584mm) rims, width usually quoted in inches.

Wheel Specification

The wheels will constitute a significant proportion of the total cost (and weight) of the bike, so it is vital that you set your budget early in the specification process. As stated previously, upgrading wheels is very straightforward, so it is important to decide whether you want "good" (relative to the rest of the bike) wheels from the start or would rather spend more on other components and procure better wheels at a later date.

The table below outlines the general cost categories of wheels to help with your budget setting.

Category	Description	Guide Price (pair)
Budget	Entry-level wheels with alloy rims	£60-£300
Premium Alloy	Typically lighter (or stronger) than above, using better grade materials for rims, spokes and hubs, often with sealed bearings.	£300-£1000
Carbon	Lighter and/or stiffer than above, also with higher grade hubs and spokes – note however that care is required over the selection of rim brake blocks with carbon braking surfaces.	£600+

At this stage, it is also important to consider the axle standard you prefer to adopt as this will drive the specification of the frame and forks; at this stage in the process, the two main options are QR skewers or thru-axles as illustrated below (dimensions are examples, note that there are several sizes and standards for thru-axles, which are explained further in the Low Level Design).

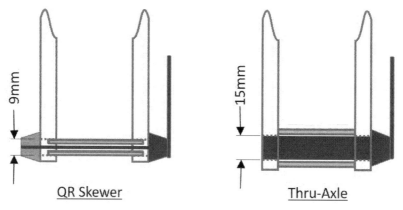

QR Skewer   Thru-Axle

- Quick Release skewers: invented by Tullio Campagnolo in 1927; standard-fit for most road bikes
- Thru-Axles: offer a stiffer interface and prevent the axle slipping during heavy braking (especially for disc brake usage).

Tyres & Wheels Specification Statement

Before proceeding, please write down your answers for the following questions:

1) What is the diameter of the wheels?
2) What is the width of the tyres?
3) What is your budget for wheels?
4) Do you have a preference for the standard of axle will you use?

Brakes

The next major component group to consider is the braking system as this will determine the type of frame and forks you will need. The key decisions are illustrated below.

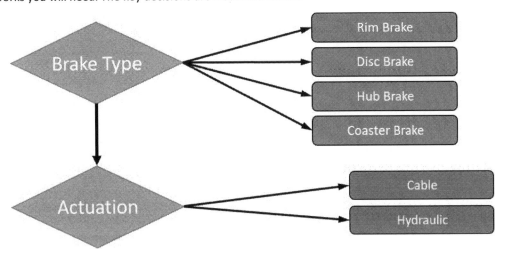

Type of Brakes

There are four types of brakes in common use as detailed below, if you have very specific needs then you may consider hub and coaster brakes, but typically the decision is between rim brakes and disc brakes. If you have chance, then I would recommend test riding both (in both dry and wet conditions) to help with your decision.

Type	Pros	Cons	Considerations
Rim	Low cost Lightweight Vast choice available	Reduced wet-weather performance Rims can wear out Rim/tyre can overheat during prolonged heavy braking	Most road bikes use side-pull calipers, whereas mountain and hybrid bikes use cantilevers (v-brakes) that have specific bosses mounted on the frame and forks.
Disc	Braking performance in all weather conditions Good choice available Discs can be replaced when worn out	Slightly heavier than rim brakes More expensive than rim brakes Prone to brake squeal	Frames & forks need integral mounting points for disc brake calipers.
Hub	Braking performance in all weather conditions	Limited choice Prone to overheating	Good for low-speed bikes in frequent wet-weather use (e.g. utility bikes).
Coaster	Powerful brakes, operated by back-pedalling	Only works with single-speed (no gears) Prone to overheating Very limited choice	Good for BMX and children's bikes.

Brake Actuation

There are two principal methods of actuating brakes:

1) Cable operated
2) Hydraulic

Cable operated brakes are most common on road bikes and are lightweight, easy to fit and maintain, and available at very competitive prices from a wide choice of manufacturers. Cable brakes are most commonly used with rim brakes but are also used for disc brakes on road, hybrid and entry-level mountain bikes. Note that over time, cables can stretch, fray (and eventually snap), and are prone to dirt-ingress.

Hydraulic brakes produce more force at the brake caliper for the same effort at the brake lever than cable brakes. They are most commonly used with disc brakes on mountain bikes and their use is increasing for new road bikes - mainly for disc brakes but also for rim brakes. More skill and effort is required to fit hydraulic brakes. If the hoses need to be shortened or internally routed then the new seals (barbs and olives) will need to be fitted and the system will need bleeding to remove air bubbles that would impair the function of the brakes. Generally, hydraulic brakes are more expensive than cable-operated brakes and the choice is more limited for road/gravel bikes (using shifters on drop handlebars). Maintenance of hydraulic brakes will include routine bleeding of the system as well as seal replacement, especially if used extensively in wet/muddy conditions.

It is also worth mentioning that certain models of brake caliper are available that have hydraulic internals (i.e. increased braking force) but are controlled by cables from the levers/shifters, thus offering a potential "best of both worlds", but choice is very limited.

Brakes Specification Statement

Before proceeding, please write down your answers for the following questions:

1) Which type of brakes will you use?
2) Which method of actuation will you use?

Gears

The aim of pedalling on a bike is to try to maintain a constant cadence (rate at which your legs go up and down) and change gear accordingly depending on the speed at which you are moving. If you were to ride on perfectly flat roads with zero wind then one gear might be sufficient, however in reality you will likely need a range of gears – but how big a range do you need?

At this stage of the specification process, we will consider the following questions:

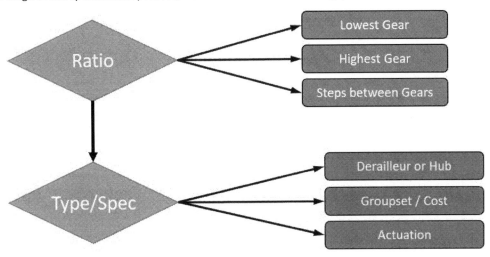

Gear Ratios

At this stage, we won't cover the details of how many chainrings or how many rear sprockets (we'll determine that during the Low Level Design). The primary decisions are:

1) **How low do you need your lowest gear?**
2) **How high do you need your highest gear?**
3) **Do you mind large jumps between gears or do you need gears very close together?**

Effective gear ratios are often quoted in gear-inches – this is a multiple of the ratio of the sprockets and the diameter of the tyre. The resulting value equates to the equivalent wheel diameter on a Penny Farthing bike (i.e. pedals connected directly to the wheel).

An effective ratio of 20 inches is a very low gear, compared to a very high gear with a ratio of 130 inches.

If you are already familiar with the number of teeth on the sprockets of your bike, you can calculate the gear-inches as follows:

$$Gear\ Inches = \frac{No.\,teeth\ on\ chainring \times tyre\ diameter\ (inches)}{No.\,teeth\ on\ cassette}$$

For a road bike with a compact chainset (50-34) and an 11-28 cassette with 700c x 25mm tyres:

The lowest gear would be: $Gear\ Inches = \frac{34\ x\ 26.5}{28} = 32.2$

The highest gear would be: $Gear\ Inches = \frac{50\ x\ 26.5}{11} = 120.5$

Cadence

Another factor to consider is your personal preference for cadence – some people like to spin the pedals more quickly than others. A cadence over 100 rpm is considered fast (spinning), whilst a cadence below 80 rpm is considered slow (mashing).

Note that if the gradient gets very steep, then it's likely that your cadence will slow down - even in your lowest gear.

To help with your selection, the graph below shows the relationship between gear-inches and road speed for different cadence rates.

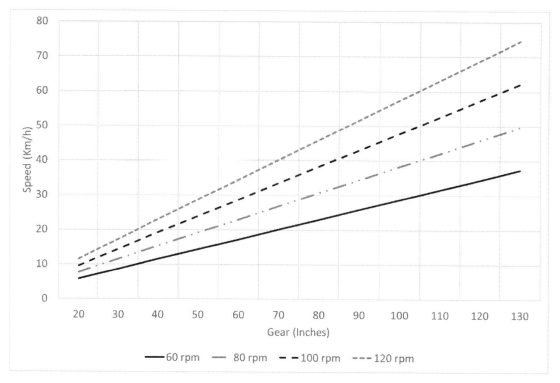

The Lowest Gear is typically used for climbing hills, so consider the terrain you intend to ride, the likely slowest speed you ride at on the inclines at your lowest cadence. Then look up these values on the above graph & pick a target low gear.

The Highest Gear is typically used for pedalling on descents, so consider the terrain you intend to ride, the likely highest speed at which you still want to be able to pedal effectively (albeit at a higher cadence) – also consider if you will be riding with a group where you will need to occasionally maintain a high speed (and not spin-out). Then look up these values on the above graph & pick a target high gear.

Then consider the **Intervals between the Gears**, for example a time-trial rider will likely want gears very close together to be able to maintain their optimum cadence across a fairly narrow speed range, whereas if you ride hilly terrain and are frequently changing gear then you may prefer wider intervals.

Types of Gears

The two main types of gears are:

Derailleur gears – whereby the chain is shifted across a range of sprockets by front and rear mechanisms;

Hub gears – whereby the gear system is contained internally within the rear hub.

It is also possible to combine the above systems to further increase the gearing range (e.g. Brompton offers an internal 3-speed hub that can be combined with a rear 2-speed derailleur – giving a total of 6 gears).

On road and mountain bikes, the most common standard is to use derailleur gears, however it is worth considering hub gears as they offer the following benefits:

- As the gears are internal, they are not subject to mud and rain, and are also protected from knocks and falls, therefore typically lasting much longer than derailleur components with less maintenance;
- As an example with Shimano's Nexus system, you can change gear whilst both stationary or moving;
- Stronger/wider chains and hubs can be used.

The disadvantages of hub gears are:

- Most systems are not able to deliver as wide a range of ratios as with a derailleur system;
- They tend to be heavier and more expensive than derailleur systems (for similar number of gears);
- Slightly less efficient (ratio of power from legs reaching the wheel);
- More fiddly and time consuming to remove the rear wheel (e.g. puncture repair);
- More expensive to repair, requiring specialist tools and skills.

How Much to Spend on the Gear System?

The major manufacturers all have families of gear systems (known collectively as "Groupsets", which also include brake levers and calipers) to suit a wide range of budgets. As the gear system includes a number of key components, it will form a significant part of the overall budget for your bike.

The following tables show a comparison of the groupsets from the major manufacturers and a rough indication of the costs (based on typical internet retailer prices at the time of writing).

(Price includes: Chainset, shifters, front mech, rear mech, cassette and chain – cable shift versions only)

The main differences as you ascend the families are:

- Weight saving through higher grade materials or more intensive manufacturing;
- Improvement in shift quality (easier to operate and more accurate shifting between gears);
- Additional features (e.g. 11-speed rather than 9 or 10-speed).

The main difference between the manufacturers is in the method of changing gear:

- Shimano road shifters have two separate paddles for up and down changing;
- SRAM road shifters use a single paddle with a "DoubleTap" mechanism;
- Campagnolo shifters use a paddle for up-shifting and a button for down-shifting.

If possible, try test-riding each of the above to see which you prefer.

Road Bikes

Shimano	SRAM	Campagnolo	Budget
		Super Record	£1500+
Dura Ace	Red	Record	£1300
		Chorus	£800
Ultegra	Force	Potenza (Athena)	£600
105	Rival	Veloce	£350
Tiagra	Apex	Centaur	£250
Sora			Typically used on entry-level whole bikes, not as separate components
Claris			

Mountain Bikes (prices excluding brakes)

Shimano	SRAM	Budget
	XX	£800+
XTR M9000	X	£700
XT M8000	GX / X9	£300
SLX M7000	NX / X7	£250
Deore M6000	X5	
Alivio M4000	X4	Typically used on entry-level whole bikes, not as separate components
Acera M3000	X3	
Altus M2000		
Tourney		

In addition to the above, Shimano also offer Zee M640 and Saint M820, which are heavier-duty products for more extreme mountain bike riding, likewise SRAM has the X0 series. SRAM also offer their 12-speed Eagle systems, which necessitate the use of their XD-Driver for the freehub (more detail on this in the Low Level Design section of the book).

Gear Actuation

The final aspect to cover at the High Level Design stage is whether you will use traditional cables or electronic controls to change gear.

Cable-operated gears are much cheaper and are available across the whole range of the major manufacturers' product families.

Electronic gears carry a slight weight premium (due to the battery) but offer the ability to programme the system to control both front and rear gear changing from one controller, as well as more precise shifting & are not prone to cable-stretch.

However, electronic systems cost around £500 more than their cable equivalents and are only available on the high-end products (e.g. Ultegra and XT).

Shimano's system is branded "Di2", SRAM's is branded "e-TAP" and "AXS"; and Campagnolo's is branded "EPS".

Gears Specification Statement

Before proceeding, please write down your answers for the following questions:

1) What is the target gear-inch for the lowest gear?
2) What is the target gear-inch for the highest gear?
3) What is your preference for the size of the interval between gears?
4) Which type of gears will you use (derailleur or hub)?
5) What is your budget for the gear system?
6) Which method of actuation will you use?

Frame and Forks

Having decided on the high level specifications for tyres, wheels, gears and brakes, you are now ready to consider the frame and forks; known together as the frameset. The purpose of this section is to enable you to filter the vast array of available framesets down to a much-reduced list that is compatible with your previous specification decisions and aligns with your budget. The key considerations are illustrated below.

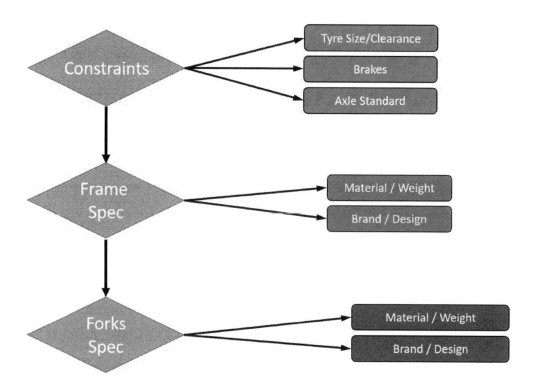

Constraints

Your high level specification decisions will now enable you to filter frameset options as follows:

Wheel Diameter: most frames are matched to a specific wheel size (although some MTB/Hybrid frames may accommodate both 650b and 29").

Tyre Clearance: this will constrain your choice if you are planning to use wider tyres than the norm for the genre of bikes; also consider if you require clearance for mudguards between the tyres and the frame and forks.

Brakes: Rim and disc brakes need different drilled/threaded mounting positions that are integral to the structure of the frame and forks; also the rear dropout width is usually 5mm wider for disc brakes (e.g. road bikes have 130mm spacing with rim brakes or 135mm spacing for disc brakes).

Axle Standards: make sure both the frame and forks align with your chosen standard (e.g. 9mm QR, 15mmx100 Front Thru-axle, etc.).

Frame Specification

The two most significant factors that will affect the price of the frame are the brand and the material.

If you are dead-set on owning a particular prestige brand then expect to pay a premium; in this case, do your research (e.g. read a number of magazine and user reviews) and spend your money wisely.

At the other end of the spectrum, you can import your own frame (e.g. direct from a Chinese factory) and make significant savings – but it's advisable to conduct your own due diligence before buying!

Regarding the decision on material, the mainstream options and budget costs are outlined below.

Material	Pros	Cons	Road	MTB (Frame only)
Steel	Usually strong, compliant for greater comfort – often used for touring bikes with panniers etc. Damage usually visible and repairable	Heavy Prone to rusting	£100-£200	£200-£400
Aluminium Alloy	Lighter than steel Damage usually visible, sometimes repairable Many road/gravel framesets have carbon forks	Alloy frames can give a harsh ride	£150-£300	£100+ (Hardtail) £500+ (full sus)
Carbon	Lighter than aluminium alloy	Damage not always visible (e.g. after a crash), can break without warning. Requires specialist repair	Entry level from £250 Prestige from £1000	£600+ (Hardtail) £1000+ (full sus)
Titanium	Optimum blend of strength, low weight and good compliance without rusting	Typically slightly heavier than carbon fibre frames Can lack stiffness for MTB	£1000+	£1000+

For mountain bikes, the initial factor that will help you filter-down the choice of frames is the amount of suspension travel you require. This may vary from zero (i.e. a hardtail) through to over 200mm for a downhill bike. At this stage, try to align to one of the following:

- Hardtail (no rear suspension)
- 100-140mm (lighter-duty / cross country)
- 140-170mm (Enduro / All Mountain)
- More than 170mm (Downhill)

Note, the above measurements refer to the vertical travel of the wheel, not the amount of compression of the spring/shock (explained further in the Low Level Design Chapter).

Road Bike Forks Specification

For road bikes, most framesets comprise a frame with a matching set of forks, although sometimes made from different materials (e.g. Alloy frame with carbon-bladed forks). When considering forks for a road bike, then follow the guidance within the above section for frames (note the budget prices above include forks).

MTB Forks Specification

With mountain bikes, suspension forks are typically sold separately from the frame and provided by specialist fork manufacturers. There are many variables with mountain bike forks, however at this stage of the specification process we will consider the following ones:

Tyre size: For optimum function and performance, the forks need to match the tyre diameter (e.g. typically 26", 27.5" or 29") and have sufficient clearance for the width of tyres specified.

Axle Standard: This needs to match the intended specification (e.g. 9mm QR, Thru-axle, Boost, etc.)

Travel: Fork travel can typically vary from 80mm for light cross country use up to over 200mm for downhill bikes. The travel of the fork will affect the overall geometry of the bike, so it's important to match the frame to the forks (i.e. fit 160mm travel forks to a frame with 160mm travel).

Severity of Use: Forks intended for light-duty riding will have narrow/lightweight stanchions, whereas downhill forks will use wider & stronger ones. Downhill forks also typically have a dual crown and longer stanchions that extend as far as the top of the steerer tube for extra strength.

Product Family: The cost of mountain bike forks varies enormously from entry-level forks through to highly specified top-of-the-range forks, the table below gives you an indication of costs for budget setting purposes.

Ranking	Key Features	Budget
Entry-Level	100-120mm travel Basic damping Light-duty use Usually 9mm QR	£100-£200
Mid-range	120-160mm travel Better damping control than above Range of use options available Usually Thru-axle	£200-£500
Specialist	140-210mm travel Advanced spring and damping control Optimum material/strength/weight to suit use Usually Thru-axle	£500+

Frameset Specification Statement

Before proceeding, please write down your answers for the following questions:

1) What material frame will you use?
2) What is your budget for the frameset (frame only for MTB)?
3) (for MTB) – specify the travel and intended use for the forks
4) (for MTB) – What is your budget for the forks?

Setting the Target Cost and Weight for the Bike

Now that you have covered the major components of the bike, you can run a first iteration for the total cost and total weight of the bike (see tables below for a guide). If either of these doesn't align with your expectations you can revisit each of the major components and modify your choices accordingly.

The following tables provide top-down estimates for road bikes and mountain bikes, please use these as a rough guide at this stage. The cost and weight estimates will be reviewed again following the Low Level Design.

(Note: "Low-Spec" in these examples is still a very capable bike)

Worked Examples – Road Bike

Component	Low Spec		Mid Spec		High Spec	
	Cost	Weight	Cost	Weight	Cost	Weight
Tyres, Tubes & Wheels	£150	2.7kg	£400	2.3kg	£1,300	2kg
Brakes & Gears	£300	2.8kg	£550	2.6kg	£1,300	2.2kg
Frameset (incl. headset)	£170	2.5kg	£550	1.7kg	£1,500	1.3kg
Bars, Stem, Saddle, Seatpost, Pedals	£130	1.5kg	£200	1.4kg	£400	1.2kg
Total	£750	9.5kg	£1,700	8kg	£4,500	6.7kg

Worked Examples – Hardtail

Component	Low Spec		Mid Spec		High Spec	
	Cost	Weight	Cost	Weight	Cost	Weight
Tyres, Tubes & Wheels	£160	4kg	£460	3.3kg	£1,000	3kg
Brakes & Gears	£340	3kg	£480	2.8kg	£1,100	2.6kg
Frame (incl. headset)	£200	2.1kg	£750	1.7kg	£1,000	1.6kg
Forks	£200	2.2kg	£460	1.9kg	£800	1.6kg
Bars, Stem, Saddle, Seatpost, Pedals	£100	1.7kg	£350	1.8kg	£700	1.7kg
Total	£1000	13kg	£2,500	11.5kg	£4,600	10.5kg

Worked Examples – Full-suspension MTB / Downhill Bike

Component	Low Spec		Mid Spec		High Spec	
	Cost	Weight	Cost	Weight	Cost	Weight
Tyres, Tubes & Wheels	£180	3.6kg	£470	3.4kg	£1,000	3.3kg
Brakes & Gears	£340	2.9kg	£480	2.8kg	£1,100	2.6kg
Frame (incl. rear shock & headset)	£800	4.0kg	£1,550	3.5kg	£3,000	3.2kg
Forks	£330	2.0kg	£500	1.9kg	£1000	1.9kg
Bars, Stem, Saddle, Seatpost, Pedals	£200	2.0kg	£350	1.7kg	£900	1.6kg
Total	£1,850	14.5kg	£3,350	13.3g	£7000	12.6kg

Everything needs to work

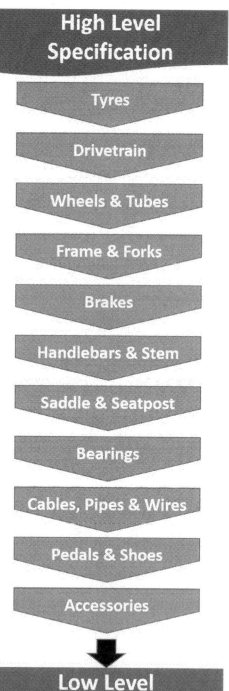

4. Low Level Design

This chapter will cover each component group in detail and guide you towards specific product selections whilst understanding the potential issues of component inter-compatibility.

The process continues, starting with the High Level Specification and working through all the component groups (in a slightly different sequence, as illustrated in the adjacent diagram) to arrive at the Low Level Specification, which will provide you with a thorough understanding of the specification and expected function of the bike as well as an accurate view of the total cost and weight.

Materials Overview

Before we launch into the component specification process, it's worth having a basic understanding of the materials commonly used for structural bike components.

- **Aluminium Alloy**, which is available in several grades:
  - 2000-series, with copper as the main additive
  - 6000-series, the most common alloy (especially 6061-grade), with magnesium and silicon as the main additives, it can also be heated treated to increase strength – designated with a "T" suffix (e.g. 6061-T6).
  - 7000-series, with zinc as the main additive and can also be heat treated.

- **Steel**, also available in many different alloys, notably for bikes:
  - Plain carbon steel,
  - Cr-Mo, alloyed with Chromium, Manganese and Molybdenum (typically 4130 grade)
  - Reynolds 631, developed from the original 531 tubing – cold-worked and air-hardened
  - Stainless Steel (e.g. Reynolds 953)

- **Titanium**, with two alloys used for bikes:
  - Grade 5: 6-4Ti (Ti-6Al-4V), has 6% aluminium and 4% vanadium.
  - Grade 9: 3-2.5Ti (Ti-3Al-2.5V), has 3% aluminium and 2.5% vanadium.

- **Carbon Fibre**, which comprises several elements within its structure and manufacture:
  - Carbon filaments, which provide the tensile strength;
  - Resin, which hold the fibres in place;
  - Pre-preg sheets, which are thin sheets containing filaments in resin;
  - Lay-up, where pre-preg sheets of differing properties are assembled in different orientations to make the desired component.

  There are four grades used for bikes, with a blend used depending on the structural needs of the components:

  - Standard Modulus (e.g. T700) – lower cost and used extensively;
  - Intermediate Modulus (e.g. T800) – stronger but more expensive;
  - High Modulus – stronger than above but more brittle;
  - Very High Modulus – even stronger but much more brittle, so used selectively away from impact zones.

In addition to material choice, a number of manufacturing technologies are also quoted as part of component specification, including:

- Double / Triple butted, where tubing is thicker at the ends than in the middle
- Hydroformed, where high-pressure fluids are used to form complex tube shapes

The table below summarises the characteristics of these structural materials.

Material	Pros	Cons	Best Use
Al-2000	High strength and hardness	Difficult to weld, corrodes easily if not painted	One-piece items such as stems
Al-6000	Highly weld-able and formable, less expensive than other alloys, good corrosion resistance	Less strength and hardness than 2000 or 7000 alloys	Most components, especially frames (6061 grade)
Al-7000	High strength and hardness, better corrosion resistance than 2000-series	Corrosion resistance and weld-ability not as good as 6000-series	Stems, sprockets, handlebars (7075 grade) Frames (7005 grade)
Plain Steel	Cheap	Not as strong as other steels	Budget bikes or components
Cr-Mo	Strong, stiff, highly weld-able	Will rust if not painted, much higher density than aluminium	Frames (also handlebars, seatposts, etc.)
R-631	Strong & stiff	Requires specialist welding Will rust if not painted	Frames
R-953	Very strong & high impact strength Corrosion resistance	Requires specialist welding High price	Frames
3-2.5Ti	Good balance of strength and low weight Corrosion resistance More malleable than 6-4Ti (e.g. for tube construction)	Requires specialist welding High price	Frames (also handlebars, seatposts, etc.)
6-4Ti	Good balance of strength and low weight Stronger than 3-2.5Ti Corrosion resistance	Less malleable and weld-able than 6-4Ti, very expensive for frame tubing Very high price	Frames
Carbon Fibre	Very good strength to weight performance, Can be created in complex shapes, Corrosion resistance Good damping properties (reduces vibration)	Product quality and capability depends on the design and manufacturer and is difficult to differentiate. Not as hard as steel.	Structural components not subject to wear

Tyres

Once again, we start the specification process with the contact points between bike and road – the tyres, which will drive the specification of the wheels and in turn the frameset. The full considerations for tyres are shown in the diagram below.

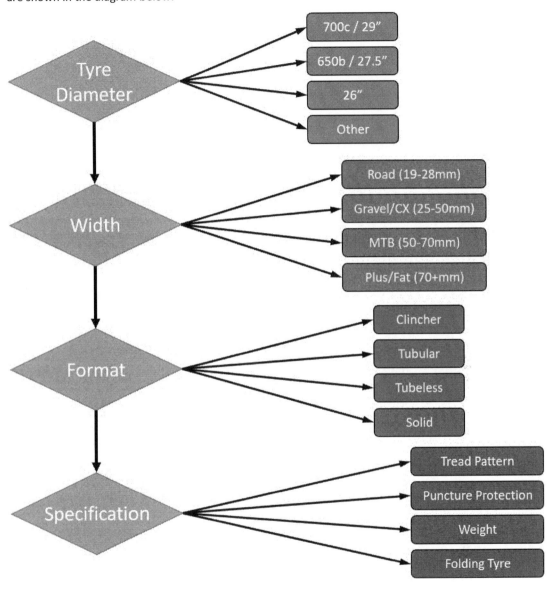

Tyre Diameter and Tyre Width were the key parameters decided during the High Level Design phase, the next level of detail now includes Tyre Format and Tyre Specification.

Tyre Format

Tyres are available in four formats, the characteristics and considerations are described below.

Format	Characteristics	Considerations
Clincher	This is the traditional tyre format with a separate tyre and inner tube.	Prone to punctures but easy to repair.
Tubular	Lightweight tyres for road racing that are glued to the wheel rim	Time consuming to fit/repair, best suited for professional cyclists with support vehicles carrying spare wheels.
Tubeless	Like a car tyre, the tyre forms an air-tight seal with the rim without the need for an inner tube. Typically a puncture-sealing liquid is added inside the tyre for that will self-repair minor holes (e.g. thorns).	Tyres and wheels both need to be compatible for tubeless use. This format is now widely used for mountain bikes as lower pressures can be run without the risk of pinch-puncturing the inner tube. They are less common for road bikes but choice is increasing. Suitability is also good for hybrid and gravel bikes although choice is limited.
Solid	Tyres constructed from a solid yet compliant material resulting in a puncture-proof solution.	Not suitable for off-road use, generally heavier than clinchers. Very limited choice but ideal for commuter bikes where a puncture might mean a missed train or meeting!

Specific notes for Tubeless Tyres

Not all tubeless tyres are equal, and there are numerous labels with inconsistent meanings.

- **UST (Uniform System Tubeless)** is a certified standard and if you choose both tyres and wheels with this marking then you should have high confidence of success in fitting and in operation, these tyres have an additional layer of butyl in the casing, which adds weight, but allows them to seal to the rim without the use of a liquid sealant.

- **Tubeless Ready/Tubeless Compatible** – are not standards but generally mean the wheels/tyres have features that enable tubeless use, however dimensions can vary between manufacturers, requiring more care and attention during installation (e.g. different layers/types of rim tape).

- **Tubeless Easy** is a marketing term used by Schwalbe which is not a certified standard but does imply specific features are included for tubeless use.

All tubeless tyres can be used with an inner tube should you need to – for example if you have a flat tyre on a ride, fitting an inner tube may enable you to continue your ride.

Tyre Specification

In order to help you get to a final shortlist of tyres to choose from, you will also need to consider the following:

Tread Pattern

-   For road tyres, typically there is very little tread unless you are looking for winter-specific tyres.
-   For MTB, there is a wide array of tread patterns, I would suggest you read specific tyre specifications and related reviews to guide you to a final selection - you may choose different tyres for front and rear.
-   Hybrid bikes will typically have a tread pattern more suitable for fast-rolling on roads than off-road grip.
-   Gravel and cyclocross tread patterns will depend on the nature of riding you intend. You will need deeper/knobbly tread for mud and grass compared to paths and bridleways.

Puncture Protection

Tyres are available with layers of reinforcing material such as Kevlar which reduce the risk of punctures, but typically increase the weight of the tyres.

Weight

I strongly recommend you to pay close attention to the weight of your tyres. The impact of reducing rotating mass at the perimeter of the wheel will having the biggest impact regarding the feel and responsiveness of the bike. But lighter tyres are potentially prone to more punctures and may wear out quicker.

Generally though, it's more cost-effective to choose higher-specification tyres and save weight than it is to obtain an equivalent weight-saving with a new set of wheels.

Folding tyres

Tyres with a bead made from a material such as Kevlar (rather than steel wire) can be folded without damaging the tyre (the use of Kevlar rather than steel also reduces weight), which makes it possible to carry a folded spare tyre with you on a ride if you wish.

Tyre Detailed Specification

Before proceeding, please write down your answers for the following questions:

1) Which format of tyres?
2) What is the specification of your tyres (tread/construction/weight)

Now you are ready to browse the shops, create a shortlist and set your budget cost and weight.

Drivetrain

The most complex component group to specify is the drivetrain system, comprising the crankset, chainrings, cassette, changer mechanism(s), shifters and chain. The sequence of specification is shown in the diagram below.

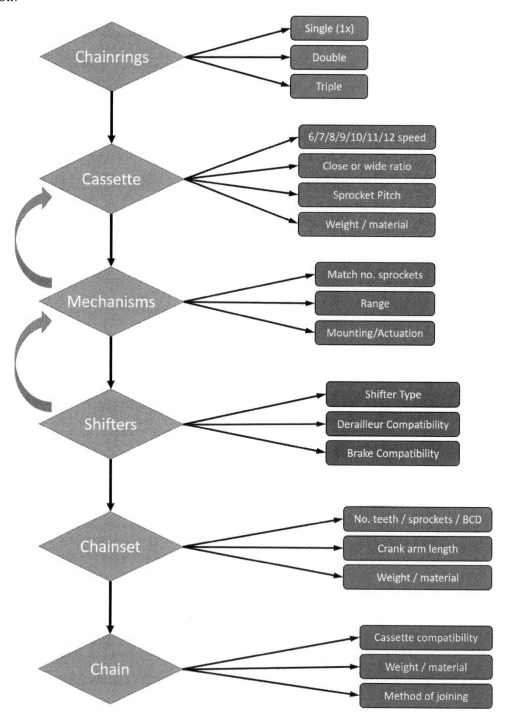

How many chainrings?

From the High Level Design phase, you should have an understanding of the range of gears you require. The next step is to determine the number of chainrings – typically, the choice is 1, 2 or 3.

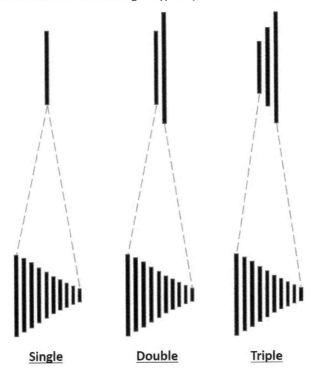

| Single | Double | Triple |

Single

- Referred to as "1x" or "one-by", this is the simplest setup, eliminates the need for a front mechanism/shifter and allows sequential use of all the gears from one shifter.
- 1x specific chainrings also have a design of alternating narrow and wide teeth that are taller than conventional chainring teeth and engage more positively with the chain and reduce occurrences of dropping the chain – especially relevant for MTB / gravel / cyclocross bikes.
- The two main drawbacks are the reduced gear range (more to follow on this) and a more excessive skew in the line of the chain leading to increased wear and shorter chain-life.
- If you are considering hub gears, then it's most likely you will use a single chainring.

Double

- This is the typical setup for a road bike, offering a good balance between ratio-range and low weight.
- Chain-line is also close to optimal if used correctly (i.e. avoiding big-big / small-small combinations)

Triple

- If you require an extreme range of gearing (e.g. on a touring bike) then a triple-chainring is the typical solution.
- The penalty is extra weight, reduced component choice and more care when selecting gears whilst riding to avoid running extreme chain-line skew.

Accommodating your choice of gear ratios

Road-going bikes: the table below shows a typical (wide) range of gear ratios for road/hybrid/gravel bikes with derailleur gears.

	1x	2x	3x
Large Chainring	42	52	50
Small Chainring	n/a	36	30
Large Rear Sprocket	42	32	32
Small Rear Sprocket	11	11	11
Highest Gear (inches)	103.7	128.4	123.5
Lowest Gear (inches)	27.2	30.6	25.5

MTB: the table below shows a typical range of gear ratios for mountain bikes (or touring bikes) with derailleur gears.

	1x	2x	3x
Large Chainring	32	36	40
Small Chainring	n/a	26	22
Large Rear Sprocket	46	40	34
Small Rear Sprocket	11	11	11
Highest Gear (inches)	80.1	90.1	100.1
Lowest Gear (inches)	19.1	17.9	17.8

Note: other ratios are available beyond those in the tables above if you wish to fine-tune your selection.

Cassettes

For derailleur systems, the cluster of rear sprockets is known as the cassette. The first step of the Low Level Design process is to determine what "speed" (how many sprockets on the cassette) you need and the interval of number of teeth between each sprocket. Cassettes are available with 5,6,7,8,9,10,11 or 12 sprockets and with varying ranges of intervals between the sprocket sizes to give wide-range gearing or close-range gearing.

Modern bikes typically have 10 or 11 speed cassettes (entry-level bikes will be 8 or 9 speed), however the growing trend is towards 12 speed cassettes for both road and mountain bikes.

If you are constrained to re-using an existing 10-speed groupset, it is possible to fit an expander sprocket (e.g. 42-teeth) to the cassette to increase its range.

Road Cassettes

For bikes that will be used mainly on the road (road bikes, hybrid bikes, and gravel bikes) the choice will typically be for one or two chainrings with a number of options available for the range of teeth on the cassette. The diagram below shows the gearing comparison for three configurations.

1) Close-ratio (11-23) cassette with 53/39 chainrings – for high-speed flat road racing;
2) Wide-ratio (11-32) cassette with 50/34 chainrings – for hilly sportive-style riding;
3) 1x11 with 11-42 cassette and 42-tooth chainring – for gravel bikes.

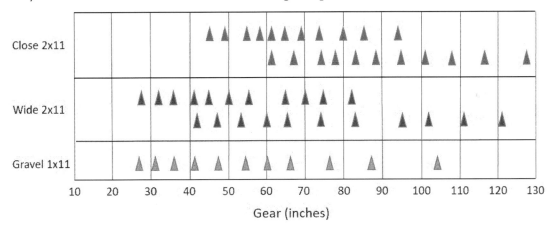

Some key observations from the above graph are:

- If your style of riding is centred on riding at 40km/h with minimal cadence variation across flat terrain, then close-ratio 2x11 gearing will be your preference.
- If you are new to cycling and want the option of low gears in case you encounter steeper hills, then choose the 2x11 wide ratios.
- If you want the simplicity and stability of a single (narrow-wide) chainring, then a wide-ratio cassette such as 11-42 coupled with a mid-size chainring such as 42T will offer all but the highest two gears of a wide-ratio 2x11 setup (a bigger chainring would improve the top end at the expense of the lowest gears if preferred).

In addition to the above, there are cassettes that fall in between Close and Wide, such as 12-25 or 11-28 if you prefer - or if you want an extra-low gear for steep hills, consider an 11-34 cassette.

MTB Cassettes

Mountain bikes are readily available in single, double and triple chainring configurations, with the trend moving towards single (1x) as the most popular format. The graph below shows the gearing comparison for three configurations.

1) 3x10 with 11-34 cassette and 40/30/22 chainrings (upper range limit for a typical long-cage mech)
2) 2x11 with 11-40 cassette and 36/26 chainrings
3) 1x11 with 11-46 cassette and 32-tooth chainring

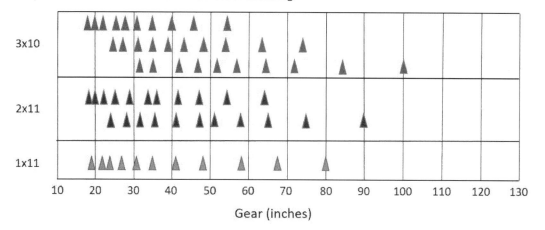

Note that the lowest gear is very similar for each of the above configurations, the main difference is the size of the high gears.

- If you intend a lot of on-road use on your MTB, then you may find the highest gear is too low with a 1x setup, in which case you will require a front derailleur/shifter and the choice is then between 2x and 3x.
- If you can live with an 80" top gear, then 1x11 eliminates the cost & weight of the front mech/shifter. (Note 1x chainrings are available with 30,32,34,36 or 38 teeth if you wish to tailor the gear-range accordingly).
- You could also consider using the SRAM XD Driver or Shimano Micro-spline freehub with a 9 or 10 tooth high gear and potentially a 12-speed cassette with a 50 or 51 tooth rear sprocket.

For example a SRAM Eagle 10-50 cassette paired with a single 34-tooth chainring will give a gear range from 18.7 through to 93.4 inches.

Cassette Sprocket Pitch

Cassette Pitch is the horizontal (axial) distance from the centre of one sprocket to the centre of the next sprocket. The pitch reduces as the number of sprockets increases and there are numerous configurations – the most common are detailed in the table below. If you keep to components within a single groupset, then you are less likely to have issues - versus attempting to mix and match!

Configuration	Specification	Limitations
Screw-on	Older style of freewheel that screws onto a threaded hub – in 5,6,7 & 8 speed	Not interchangeable with more modern freehub designs
Shimano/SRAM 9-speed	Pitch = 4.35mm	Not compatible with Campagnolo 9-speed
Shimano/SRAM 10-speed	Pitch = 3.95mm, common across road & MTB	Not compatible with Campagnolo 10-speed
Shimano/SRAM 11-speed (Road)	Shimano Pitch = 3.74mm SRAM Pitch = 3.72mm	Not compatible with 11-speed MTB
Shimano/SRAM 11-speed (MTB)	Pitch = 3.9mm	Not compatible with 11-speed Road
Shimano/SRAM 12-speed	Pitch = 3.65mm	SRAM with XD Driver Shimano with Micro Spline freehub
Campagnolo	9-speed = 4.55mm 10-speed = 4.15mm 11-speed = 3.85mm	Campagnolo cassettes use a different spline configuration to Shimano & SRAM requiring a different freehub
SRAM XD Driver	Alternative design of freehub that enables the use of SRAM cassettes with a 10-tooth high gear or a 9-tooth from e*thirteen	Limited range of wheels/hubs

Cassette Weight / Material

As you go up the "league table" of groupsets, as well as costing more, the weight of cassettes reduces through the use of lighter materials and more complex manufacturing processes. The table below gives an indication of the magnitude of weight variation across a number of SRAM cassettes (but there is typically an even bigger variation in cost from bottom to top!). Note also that aluminium sprockets, although much lighter, will wear much faster than steel ones.

Road			MTB		
Red (11-25)	Force (11-25)	Rival (11-25)	XG1199 (10-42)	XG1180 (10-42)	PG1130 (11-42)
151g	247g	260g	268g	315g	538g

Gear Changing Mechanisms

From the High Level Specification, you should be clear whether you will be using derailleur gears or hub gears - both of which will be covered in more detail in this section.

Also from the High Level Specification, you should have a target model range in mind for budget purposes – this will constrain your selection of mechanisms, but there will still be options to consider which are detailed below.

Front Derailleur

The purpose of the front derailleur (mech) is to guide the path of the chain to the selected front chainring. As you operate the mechanism it diverts the path to the adjacent chainring and so affects a gear change.

When choosing a front derailleur, the following parameters need to be considered:

- **Road or MTB**
  - Gear shifters on road bikes typically pull the gear cable a different distance per gear change compared to MTB shifters, so general advice is to use designated road bike mechs on road bikes and MTB mechs for mountain bikes, unless you have a clear understanding of respective cable-pull ratios.
- **Frame Mounting**
  - Braze-on means the frame has a mounting plate already attached for the front mech, this is typically used on road bikes;
  - Direct-mount (in either high or low variants) also has a mounting plate on the frame but in a different orientation to braze-on, this is typically used on mountain bikes;
  - Band-on means there is no bracket on the frame, but you need to match the diameter of the band on the mech to the external diameter of the seat tube (or use shims if possible);
  - E-Type – an older standard whereby the front mech is also attached to the bottom bracket;
  - Note: you can use a separate mounting bracket with a braze-on mech.
- **Cable routing**
  - Typically, the gear cable on a road bike passes under the bottom bracket and pulls downwards on the front mech – this is termed "bottom pull".
  - Conversely, the gear cable on a mountain bike is usually routed along the top tube and pulls upwards on the front mech – this is termed "top pull".
  - Some front mechs have cable routing and/or pulleys to be able to accommodate both types.
- **Chainring quantity and tooth-count**
  - Match the front mech to the quantity and size of the chainrings – check the specifications cover both the largest and smallest chainrings as well as the maximum intervals between chainrings.
- **Speed**
  - Match the speed description of the front mech to the number of sprockets on the rear cassette as this will determine the width of the chain and hence front mech spacing.
- **Swing**
  - Most road bikes have a "bottom swing" action, where the shifting mechanism sits above the cage and chainrings.
  - Some mountain bikes have a "top swing" action, where the mechanism is below the cage giving more clearance for suspension arms and bottle cages etc. Fitting a Top Swing mech on road bike can lead to clearance issues with the rear tyre.
  - A newer standard for mountain bikes is "side swing", whereby the cable enters from the front and the mechanism is away from the rear wheel or suspension components.

Rear Derailleur

The purpose of the rear derailleur (mech) is two-fold:

1) To guide the chain to the selected sprocket, and hence change gear;
2) To maintain tension on the chain across the whole range of gears.

When choosing a rear derailleur, the following parameters need to be considered:

- **Road or MTB**
  - o Gear shifters on road bikes typically pull the gear cable a different distance per gear change compared to MTB shifters, so general advice is to use designated road bike mechs on road bikes and MTB mechs for mountain bikes, unless you have a clear understanding of respective cable-pull ratios.
- **Speed**
  - o Match the speed description of the rear mech to the number of sprockets on the rear cassette, unless you have a clear understanding of respective cable-pull ratios.
- **Largest rear sprocket**
  - o Make sure the rear mech can accommodate the largest sprocket on the cassette (although you can buy a longer hanger or a longer B-screw).
- **Total teeth difference**
  - o Rear mechs are typically available in different lengths (short cage, medium cage and long cage). Calculate the difference in teeth in between the chainrings and add to the difference between smallest and largest sprockets on the cassette to get the total difference that the rear mech needs to accommodate, then choose the relevant cage length.
  - o E.g. if a rear derailleur has a limit of 39 teeth, it can support the following:
    - ▪ 1x11: 11-46 has difference of 35T, so no issue
    - ▪ 2x11: 36/26 front = 10T, 11-40 rear = 29T, total difference = 39T – on the limit
    - ▪ 3x10: 40/30/22 front = 18T, therefore the limit for rear = 21T such as 11-32
- **Clutch**
  - o Modern MTB derailleurs have a clutch feature that applies additional tension to the chain to reduce chain-bounce over rough terrain - worth considering for a gravel bike.
- **Frame attachment**
  - o The majority of modern bikes use a sacrificial (can be replaced if damaged) hanger bracket for the rear mech, which is normally supplied with the frame.
  - o Note also that there is a newer standard of mounting termed "Direct Mount" (yet another use of this term!), whereby a different shape hanger bracket is used that has more rearwards offset. The hanger brackets are normally provided with the frame and most modern rear derailleurs can be converted between conventional and direct-mount standards.

Limitations to Note:

If you wish to build a gravel bike with 1x gearing and drop handlebars, the largest standard-fit rear sprocket you can use will be:

- o Shimano: 42T (GRX), 34T (Ultegra R8000, Tiagra 10-speed) or 32T (105 / Ultegra 6800)
- o SRAM: 42T (Apex/Rival/Force), 32T (Red)
- o Campagnolo: 32T (Potenza, Chorus), 29T (Record 12-speed)

Hub Gears

If your preference is for hub gears, there are two main options to consider:

1) Geared hub only (no derailleur);
2) Geared hub with additional rear cassette and derailleur (limited choice).

The main manufacturers of hub gears include:

- **Sturmey Archer**: offering a range from 2-speed, 3-speed, 4-speed, 5-speed & 8-speed;

- **Shimano**: offering 3-speed, 8-speed & 11-speed;

- **Rohloff**: offering a 14-speed hub with a gear range of 500%;

- **NuVinci**: offering a continuously variable hubs with a range of up to 380%;

- **SRAM**: offering 2-speed & 3-speed hubs.

The key factors to consider when selecting the hub are:

- Whether you want to buy a complete wheel or a separate hub (and build the wheel yourself or have a custom-build from a wheel-builder);
- Total cost of the wheel (the price of geared hubs ranges from tens to thousands of pounds depending on make and spec);
- Gear ratio range (including chainring size, sprocket size and internal gearing);
- Actuation method – whether you prefer a cable shift or electronic, which will impact the price of the hub.

Chainset

The chainset comprises the following components:

- Right-hand crank arm, this can also include an integral axle and mounting for the chainring(s);
- Left-hand crank arm;
- Chainring(s) and bolts;

If the axle/spindle is not integral with the right-hand crank arm then this is usually part of the bottom bracket bearing assembly – covered in later section of this book.

Note: the term "crankset" usually means the two crank arms without the chainring(s) - but not always!

Chainring Compatibility

It is essential that you choose a chainset that supports both the number of chainrings and the number of teeth to deliver your desired gear ratios. The most commonly available chainsets and their configurations are listed below.

Usage	Designation	Teeth	Notes
Road Double	Sub-compact	48/32 48/31 46/30	Manufacturers include: Shimano (GRX), FSA, Praxis Works and AbsoluteBlack
	Standard	53/39	Commonly available from most manufacturers
	Compact	50/34	
	Semi-compact	52/36	
	CX (Cyclocross)	46/36	
Road Triple	Standard	50/39/30	
Road/CX Single	1x	38,40,42,44, 46,48,50,52	Limited choice of chainsets (e.g. SRAM, Shimano GRX))
MTB Single	1x	30,32,34	36 & 38 chainrings often available
MTB Double 10-speed	2x (10-speed)	38/24	Typically used with a narrower ratio cassette
MTB Double 11-speed	2x (11-speed)	34/24, 36/26 38/28	Typically used with a wider ratio cassette
MTB Triple	3x (10-speed)	40/30/22 42/32/24	Typically used with a narrower ratio cassette

A parameter you will also need to consider if you are going to source separate chainring(s) is how the chainring(s) mount to the crank arm. The two common options are:

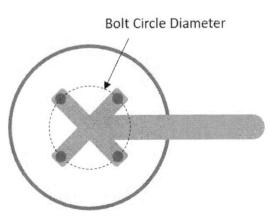

Bolt Circle Diameter

1) **Bolt-on**, whereby the chainring(s) bolt to the crankarm.
   Note: take care regarding the Bolt Circle Diameter (BCD), which the reference distance of the chainring bolts to the centreline of the crank axle. Different BCDs are used depending on the size of the chainrings and the manufacturer.

2) **Direct Mount** (yet another use of this term!), used mainly with 1x11 chainrings, whereby the chainring has an internal spline and mounts to the centre of the crank arm.

A further option to consider is whether to use an oval or a round chain ring - round ones are the norm, but some claim benefits in power output from oval rings - I suggest you do your own research before believing the marketing hype.

Crankarm Length

The next factor to consider is the length of the crank arms; the majority of cranksets are available in the following lengths (note: other length cranks are available but are not widely available):

- 165mm
- 170mm
- 172.5mm (less common for MTB)
- 175mm

Longer crank arms give more leverage but are harder to spin as fast as shorter crank arms, so this needs to be taken into consideration with your gearing selection.

The general principle is that taller people should use longer crank arms but there are no definitive rules as it will depend on factors such as relative limb-length, flexibility and muscle tone. The table below is a VERY ROUGH GUIDE – please do you own research before buying your crankset (it's expensive if you need to change!)

Height	Crank Arm Length
Less than 170cm	165mm
170-177.5cm	170mm
177.5-185mm	172.5mm
More than 185cm	175mm

Bottom Bracket / Axle Type

Cranksets are available in three different axle sizes:

1) Older-style three-piece cranksets with a 17-22mm diameter axle, typically incorporated into a cartridge bottom bracket and used with a threaded bottom bracket (refer to section on Bottom Brackets for more details).
2) 24mm diameter axle two-piece crankset, such as Shimano Hollowtech II, SRAM GXP and Campagnolo Ultra-torque.
3) 30mm diameter axle, two-piece crankset usually referred to as BB30.

Ideally, you should match the crankset with the frame's bottom bracket (e.g. SRAM GXP with threaded BB or SRAM BB30 crankset with PressFit 30 BB), however there is a variety of bottom brackets and adapters available to allow you to match up your preferred crankset with your frame choice.

Crankset Material / Weight

As with most components on a bike, there is a sliding scale as you spend more money on the crankset, the weight reduces through the use of more exotic materials and manufacturing processes – as illustrated with SRAM road cranksets below.

Product	Weight	Materials
Apex	890g	Aluminium Alloy
Rival	873g	Aluminium Alloy
Force	697g	Carbon arms, alloy spider
Red	557g	Hollow carbon arms, alloy spider

Chainline

If you stick with standard components and a single groupset, then chainline shouldn't be an issue. If you mix-and-match components, then you need to check your final setup will work as intended.

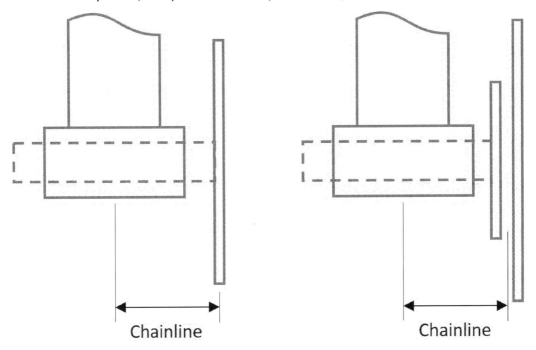

The Chainline is measured from the centre of the bottom bracket to the centre of the chainring (for single and triple or the midpoint between the chainrings of a double).

Typical measurements are:

- Road bike chainline = 43.5mm;
- Mountain bike chainline = 49mm (Boost = 52mm, Super-boost = 56mm)

Care is required if you source chainrings separately, whereby spacing washers may be required to obtain the correct dimension.

If you choose to use a Boost rear hub (148mm axle) then the chainline will need to increase by approx. 3mm accordingly.

Chains

The most fundamental parameter for the chain is to match it to the number of sprockets on the cassette (i.e. use a 10-speed chain with a 10-speed cassette).

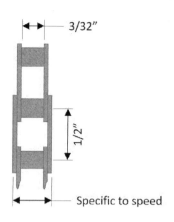

The pitch (distance between each link) of a bike chain is constant at ½" for all modern bikes. The inner width of the chain is also constant at $^3/_{32}$" for all modern bikes with derailleur gears (wider chains are available for single speed bikes). The key variable for derailleur chains is the outer width, which reduces as the speed increases (i.e. 11-speed chains are narrower than 10-speed chains).

You can run (sub-optimally) a 10-speed cassette with an 11-speed chain, but not vice versa.

As you'd expect, more money buys you a slightly lighter chain with features such as hollow pins.

A further difference to consider is the manufacturer of the chain and the different approaches for joining the chain together, the main manufacturers' chains are detailed below (note that there are many other chain suppliers that you could consider).

Manufacturer	Method of joining	Limitations
KMC	Split-link connector	11-speed links are not recommended for re-use (i.e. replace with new link)
Shimano	Connector pin (newest chains have split-links)	Pins not reusable (split the chain at a different point and use a new pin).
SRAM	Split-link connector	Not recommended for re-use
Campagnolo	Connector pin	Specific Campagnolo tool required (different tool for 10-speed and 11-speed). Pins not reusable.

Note: there are no major differences between chains for road bikes and chains for mountain bikes. KMC and Shimano do not differentiate, whilst SRAM sells specific chains for both disciplines.

Chain Length
Make sure you buy a chain that is long enough!!
An easy mistake to make if you are not careful, especially with wide-range cassettes. For derailleur bikes (where there is approx. 180° of chain-wrap) the formula for chain length is:

$$No. Links = 2 + (4 \ x \ chainstay) + \frac{biggest\ sprocket + biggest\ chainring}{2}$$

Where "chainstay" = distance from centre of BB to centre of rear axle, measured in inches

Note: for 1x drivetrains, it is recommended to add two additional links to the above calculation.

Note also, for a single-speed bike with a large chain ring (much more than 180° wrap) and a small sprocket the above equation is not suitable, there are however a number of internet-based calculators you could use.

Gear Shifters

There are a number of different types of gear shifter, depending on handlebar style:

Drop Handlebars:

- Shifters that are combined with brake levers (also called "Brifters");
- Bar-end shifters, which can also be used with aero bars on time-trial bikes;
- Downtube shifters found on vintage road bikes.

For cable-operated gears, you will need to choose just one of the above. For electronically controlled gears, it is possible to fit both combined gear/brake levers with aero-bar shifters.

Flat / MTB handlebars:

- Trigger shifters;
- Twist-grip shifters.

It will be a matter of personal preference regarding the type you choose but note that the widest choice will be available for trigger shifters for MTB/Hybrid and combined gear and brake levers for road/gravel bikes.

Compatibility

Your budget will most likely determine the specification of the shifters, leaving you to decide your preference on manufacturer (with their different methods of shifting as described during the High Level Design).

The most important aspect is to match the number of gears on the shifter with the respective derailleur. If you wish to use a triple chainring, then make sure the front shifter is specified accordingly (some front shifters have a switch that allow you to choose between two and three chainrings).

If you choose all your drivetrain components from a single groupset, then you should be free from compatibilities issues. Mixing components, especially shifters and mechanisms, is likely to lead to issues unless you are sure the cable-pull-ratios match suitably. Similarly, care is required to match the pull-ratio of the brake lever with the brake caliper – not an issue if matching within a groupset but care is required if using different manufacturers for shifters and brake calipers or mixing road and MTB components.

For example, on Shimano road brakes, newer models use SLR-EV (Shimano Linear Response, found on models whereby the cable runs under the bar tape e.g. Dura Ace, Ultegra & 105), which have a different cable pull ratio to older brakes (and other manufacturers) and therefore need matching to SLR-EV brake calipers.

Electronic Shift

If you are planning to specify electronic shift (e.g. Di2), then ensure you include all the constituent parts, such as:

- Junction units to match your frame (some frames allow for built-in junction units)
- Wireless modules if required (e.g. Shimano's EW-WU111 for use with their phone app etc.)
- Sufficient wires of appropriate length
- Battery and holder (e.g. frame mount or seatpost adapter)
- Battery charger

Gear Lever Mounting

There are a number of options for mounting flat-bar gear and brake levers to consider.

1) Separate levers, each with their own clamp – this is usually termed "Bar Mount";
2) Levers that share a single handlebar mount – there are various standards, such as:
    - Shimano uses: I-Spec A, I-Spec B, and I-Spec II;
    - SRAM uses MMX (Matchmaker X), which will hold three components (brake, gear & dropper seatpost remote control).

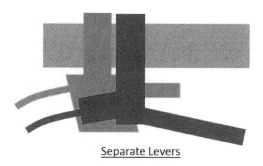

Separate Levers

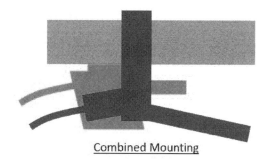

Combined Mounting

Hydraulic Road Shifters

The trend is increasing for the use of hydraulic brakes on road and gravel bikes but the choice of shifters is limited (and as a result the costs are much higher than for cable shifters).

Shimano offers DuraAce R9120/R170, Ultegra R8020/8070 (replacing RS785/685), GRX and 105-series R7020 (replacingRS505).

SRAM offers hydraulic shifters throughout: Red, Force, Rival and Apex options.

Campagnolo offers hydraulic shifters for Super Record Record, Chorus and Potenza options.

Drivetrain Detailed Specification

Before proceeding, please write down your answers for the following questions:

1) How many chainrings/teeth?
2) What speed and teeth range of cassette (and hence chain)?
3) Are you going with a single groupset – if so which one, if not then specify separately
4) What length cage do you need for the rear mech?
5) Cable or hydraulic brakes?
6) What is the length of the crank arms?
7) Are there any factors you need to take into account when building the bike (e.g. chainline)
8) How many links do you need for the chain?
9) What mounting system will you specify for flat-bar shifters/levers?

Now you are ready to browse the shops, create a shortlist and set your budget cost and weight.

Wheels and Inner tubes

The most noticeable weight-savings on a bike are on the components that rotate as they impact the acceleration and responsiveness of the bike as well as the overall weight when climbing. The wheels will also form a significant part of the overall cost of the bike. This section of the Low Level Design will cover the relevant decisions for wheels and also inner tubes (if needed) as illustrated below.

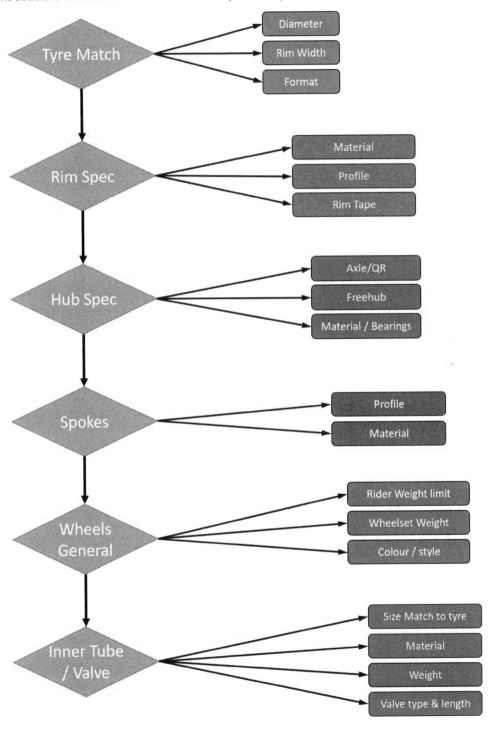

Wheel Size and Tyre Match

The chosen specification of tyres will help you filter your wheel selections as follows:

- **Diameter** – ensure you match the ISO measurements (e.g. 622mm for road bikes);

- **Width** – the width of the rim needs to align with the intended tyre width (tyres are typically wider than the rim but guidelines are provided by the tyre manufacturers for min/max rim width);
    - Road rims typically have an internal rim width of 13-20mm, e.g. 622 x 15c;
    - Gravel/hybrid rims will be around 15-23mm, e.g. 622 x 19c;
    - MTB rims will be in the range of 20-40mm, e.g. 584 x 30c;

- **Format** – if you intend to run tubular tyres, then the wheel must also be tubular specific, if you intend to run tubeless, then the wheels must state UST, tubeless ready/compatible or similar.

Off-the-shelf or custom-build?

A key decision is whether you are going to buy off-the-shelf wheels or have your wheels custom-built (you may even choose to build your own). Although there is a vast range of off-the-shelf wheels available, you may still not be able to find the right combination of rim, hub and spokes, in which case you may then choose to go down the custom-build route.

The following sections will give you further insight into rims, hubs and spokes which should provide you with sufficient information to make your component choices whichever route you choose.

Rim Specification

Road bike rims

The majority of road bike rims are made from aluminium alloy, more expensive rims use carbon fibre. Carbon fibre rims either have alloy-inlay braking tracks (so can use regular brake blocks) or are entirely constructed from carbon fibre (and therefore require carbon-specific brake blocks – or use disc brakes). Carbon fibre is typically lighter and stiffer than aluminium alloy but wears out faster, especially if subject to grime off the roads (don't use carbon rims with rim brakes on a winter or gravel bike!).

The next factor to consider is the depth profile of the rim.

- Deep section rims (50mm or more) are more aerodynamic than shallow rims and are typically used for higher speeds on relatively flat terrain. Deep rims can cause bike instability in cross-winds.
- Shallow rims (30mm or less) tend to be lighter than deep section rims and are therefore more suited for climbing, they are also less impacted by cross-winds.
- Mid-section rims are typically in the range of 30-50mm and offer a compromise between deep and shallow.

Mountain bike rims

Rims for mountain bikes cover a wide spectrum of profiles from narrow and lightweight rims for cross-country use through to wide and heavy-duty rims for downhill racing. The vast majority of rims are made from aluminium alloy, although carbon rims are also available.

Rim Tape

Some wheel rims do not have access holes for spoke nipples and are therefore by nature air-tight and smooth, thus not requiring rim tape for use with either inner tubes or going tubeless.

If you are going to use inner tubes, then most suitable rim tapes will work without issue.

If you are going tubeless (and the rims have spoke-access holes) then you will need to use a rim tape that is specifically made for tubeless installations (e.g. Stan's No Tubes). As a word of caution, you may read articles advocating the use of electrical tape or Gorilla/Duct tape – my recommendation (from personal experience) is not to use these tapes; electrical tape will deform and leak under pressure, the adhesive on Gorilla tape can make subsequent tyre removal extremely difficult.

Hub Specification

The options for hubs include:

- Hub width;
- Axle standard;
- Freehub type and specification;
- Hub material;
- Hub bearings.

Axle Standards

There are several standards of axle in mainstream use, as detailed in the following table.

Standard	Dropout Width	Typical Use	Considerations
Quick Release (9mm Front) (10mm Rear)	100mm Front 130mm Rear 135mm Rear (disc)	Rim brake road bikes Older / entry-level MTB Hybrid bikes	Fine for general use Potential issues with axle slippage & misalignment with disc brakes.
Thru-Axle (Front)	12mm x 100mm 15mm x 100mm 20mm x 100mm	Mountain bikes & newer disc brake road/gravel bikes	Eliminates axle slippage, adds stiffness to bike
Thru-Axle (Rear)	12mm x 142mm		
Thru-Axle (Front Boost)	15mm x 110mm 20mm x 110mm	Mountain bikes	Required for wider tyres (e.g. Plus or Fat), also enable the use of stiffer hubs
Thru-Axle (Rear Boost)	12mm x 148mm		
Thru-Axle (Rear Downhill)	12mm x 150mm 12mm x 157mm	Downhill MTB	

Many hubs/wheelsets can be fitted with adaptors that enable them to be converted between (some of) the above options (e.g. to convert between 100x9mm QR and 100x15mm Thru-axle, or 135x10mm QR and 142mm Thru-axle).

Axles & Skewers

The subject of axles and skewers is also a minefield with different lengths and threaded sections required for different frames and forks. The table below is a guide only. For thru-axles, if your frame/forks are not supplied with an axle then check the specification regarding length and thread pitch carefully before you buy the axles.

Use	Skewer / Axle Length	Notes
QR skewer front wheel	100mm plus dropout thickness + thread to engage with acorn nut	
QR skewer rear wheel	130mm plus dropouts and mech hanger + thread to engage with acorn nut	Rim brakes
	135mm plus dropouts and mech hanger + thread to engage with acorn nut	Disc brakes
Front Thru-axle	100mm plus 1x dropout + threaded section	Typical thread: M12 x 1.5mm pitch M12 x 1.75mm pitch M15 x 1.5mm pitch
Front Thru-axle (Boost)	110mm plus 1x dropout + threaded section	Typical thread: M12 x 1.5mm pitch M15 x 1.5mm pitch
Rear Thru-axle	142mm plus dropouts and mech hanger + thread to engage with nut	Wide range of standards available (e.g. E-Thru, Scott, Maxle) – check carefully
Rear Thru-axle (Boost)	148mm plus dropouts and mech hanger + thread to engage with nut	Wide range of standards available – check carefully
Rear Thru-axle (Downhill)	157mm plus dropouts and mech hanger + thread to engage with nut	Wide range of standards available – check carefully

Also pay attention to the **weight** of skewers and axles, for example:

- Typical road bike skewers weigh 130g/pair, but a lightweight set weighs 44g;
- A standard 15mm Thru-axle weighs 90g, a lightweight (stealth) axle weighs 40g or less.

Freehubs

Freehubs are usually supplied as part of a wheelset or the rear hub, but different standards are available, the common ones being:

1) **Shimano/SRAM compatible** – these will typically fit all 9,10 and 11 speed cassettes from Shimano, SRAM and many other compatible makes with a smallest sprocket of 11-teeth;
2) **Campagnolo compatible** – for use with Campagnolo cassettes;
3) **XD Driver** – for use with cassettes with a 9 or 10-tooth smallest sprocket.
4) **Shimano Micro Spline** – for use with Shimano 12-speed cassettes

Freehubs are also available separately and can (not always) be interchanged to suit different cassettes.

Another aspect of freehubs is the quantity of **engagement points**, i.e. how many degrees of rotation before pawls engage on the ratchet – it is measured typically as the number of times the ratchet engages over one revolution of the freehub. A value of 18 engagement points is low, compared to a high value of 72 engagement points. The higher the number, the more responsive the bike will feel when accelerating.

The final point to consider with freehubs is the **sound** they make. Some are much louder than others and if you are riding a long way it helps if you like the sound of your freehub – the best source of information is probably on YouTube!

Hub Material and Bearings

Hubs can vary in cost from a few pounds to over a thousand pounds a pair, the factors that drive the cost include:

- **Hub body material**: ranging from entry-level aluminium alloy hubs, through more advanced grades of aluminium alloy to the much more expensive hubs using titanium and also carbon fibre. Typically, weight reduces (or strength increases) with more expensive materials. For heavy-duty use (e.g. gravity MTB), high-spec steel may be used.

- **Axle material**: ranging from steel axles for entry-level hubs, with higher-end hubs using a range of aluminium (lightweight), titanium (balance of strength with low weight) or high-spec steel for ultimate strength and stiffness.

- **Bearings** are available in two formats, traditional cup-and-cone with loose bearings (used by Shimano across the range) or cartridge systems that need replacing when worn or contaminated with dirt. Each format has their own advantages and disadvantages and both are available through the price range of hubs.
  More money typically buys better specification sealing systems (to keep dirt and moisture out) as well as bearings produced to a higher ABEC (bearing standard) specification and more advanced materials. Top of the range are ceramic bearings, which generally roll smoother and last longer than steel bearings.

Spokes

The first question with spokes is: "how many?"

The second question is: "which pattern?"

Road bikes with rim brakes typically use a **radial pattern** of around 16-20 spokes for the front wheel. Rear wheels usually have a cross-laced pattern (but sometimes just on the drive side with the non-drive side using a radial pattern) with 20-24 spokes.

Mountain bikes and road bikes with disc brakes use a **cross-laced** pattern with typically around 28-36 spokes on both wheels.

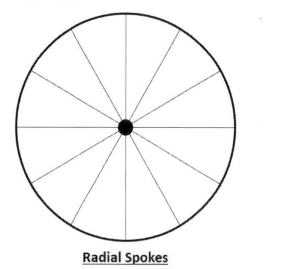
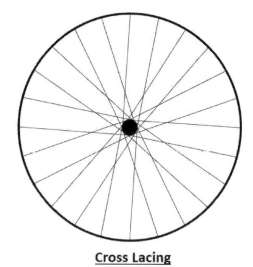

Radial Spokes   **Cross Lacing**

Other aspects to consider are:

- **Spoke profile** – to save weight, the thickness of the spoke can be reduced over the middle length of the spoke – known as "double butted" – i.e. both ends thicker than the middle.
- **Blade profile** – to improve aerodynamics, spokes can be flattened to a blade profile over their middle section.
- **Spoke Material** – most modern spokes are made from stainless steel, although titanium spokes are available and some designs also use aluminium.
- **Nipple Material** – for less weight, aluminium is used; for increased durability, brass is used.

Wheels – General Considerations

In summary for wheels, and their constituent parts as described above, consider the following:

Rider weight limit: Ensure you stay within the limits recommended by the wheel manufacturer.

Wheelset weight: saving weight on the wheels will improve the responsiveness and acceleration of the bike far more than an equivalent weight reductions on non-rotating parts, but don't compromise the strength of the wheels for your intended use of the bike (especially for heavy off-road riding).

Colour / Style: Wheels have a high visual impact, so pay attention to the colour and style of the wheels.

Inner tubes and valves

Firstly, for inner tubes, match the size of the inner tube to the tyre diameter and width.

Inner Tube Material

The majority of inner tubes are made from butyl rubber, another option is to use latex. Latex tubes are typically lighter and give a smoother ride as they are more compliant than butyl tubes. Latex tubes are more prone to damage during installation and also lose pressure over time faster than butyl, thus requiring more frequent (i.e. daily) tyre-inflation.

Inner Tube Weight

If you are after cost-efficient weight saving on a road bike, then standard inner tubes (typically 200g/pair) can be swapped for lightweight inner tubes weighing as little as 100g/pair (such as Continental Supersonic) - but do your research as thinner tubes are more prone to punctures and the effects of heat build-up under heavy rim-braking.

Valve Standards

There are two mainstream standards of valve:

1) **Schrader valves**, as used on cars, which tend to be used for lower pressure tyres. The valve diameter is 8mm, so check the hole in the rim is large enough.
2) **Presta valves** are used for higher pressures, and are typically used on road bikes and also as tubeless valves; the valve diameter is 6mm.

Valve Length

Inner Tubes are available with different length Presta valve stems. If you are using deeper section rims, then ensure the valve stem is long enough to protrude through the rim such that you can attach a pump. (Note: also make sure that any spare tubes you carry also have valves that are long enough!!!)

Note that tubeless valves are also available in a variety of lengths – ensure you match the length of the valves to the depth of the rim and enough length to attach a pump.

Wheels & Inner Tubes Detailed Specification

Before proceeding, please write down your answers for the following questions:

1) What is the rim width and depth?
2) Are you buying complete wheels or building your own?
3) Do you have any particular specification requirements for the hubs?
4) Do you have any particular specification requirements for the spokes?
5) Do you have any colour / style preferences?
6) What is the inner tube material, valve-type/length and target weight?

Now you are ready to browse the shops, create a shortlist and set your budget cost and weight.

Frame and Forks

The decisions during the High Level Design will have helped you filter down the vast array of framesets to a much smaller list of suitable options. The following sections will guide you to filter-down even further to arrive at a short-list.

The diagram below applies to all types of bike; for mountain bikes there are additional considerations which will be considered later in this chapter.

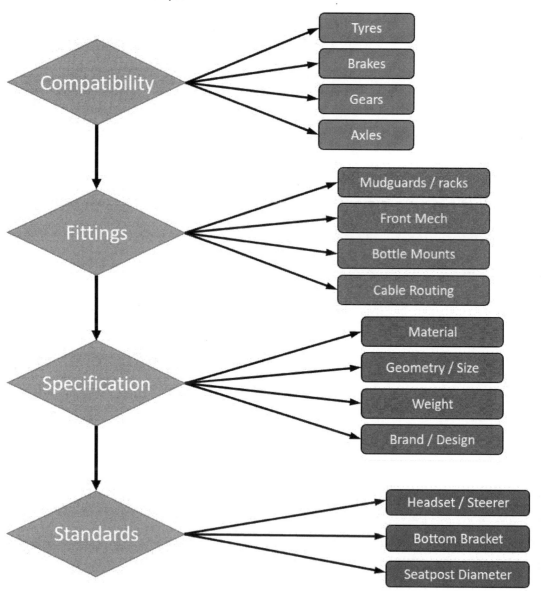

Compatibility

The High Level Design chapter reviewed the compatibility constraints for tyre size, brake type and axle type. There is one further consideration that may eliminate frames from your list, which is the maximum size of chainring that will fit, especially if using a 1x drivetrain.

As illustrated opposite, space is tight in the region where the chain-stays meet the bottom bracket, especially with wider tyres and a larger chainring running closer in-board on a 1x setup versus a 2x setup.

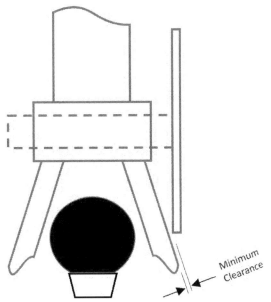

Check the small-print on frame specifications to see if there is a constraint that will be impacted by your gearing choice.

This situation is most likely on a 1x gravel/adventure/cyclocross bike as the chainring will typically be bigger than on a mountain bike, and the tyres will be wider than on a road bike.

Fittings

The next factor to consider are the fittings you require on the frame, these include:

Mudguards / Racks

Mudguards are available that fasten to the bike without bolts, but if you are after a more secure fitting then the frame will need to have specific threaded mounting points.

Similarly, if you intend to fit racks for touring then you will need mounting points on the frame.

Front Mech

This is not normally a limiting factor for frame selection, but you'll need to match the front mech mounting to the frame, whether braze-on/direct-mount or band-on – check also the seat tube diameter for band-on. Also check for tyre clearance (chain-stay length) if using a bottom-swing front mech.

Bottle Cage Mounts

Frames typically have threaded mounts for attaching bottle cages. Check the quantity of mounts on the frame to make sure it aligns with your preference. Most road bikes have two sets of mounts, but smaller-size frames sometimes only have one set.

Cable Routing

Brake and gear cables/hoses/wires can either be routed internally through specific holes in the frame or externally via guide bosses. Internal routing is neater but usually harder to install; hydraulic hoses need disconnecting to route through the frame/forks and bleeding afterwards.

The ultimate in cable routing results in totally concealed cables within the handlebar/stem assembly (see later chapter for handlebar low level design).

If you are planning to use electronic gear shifting, then check the frame supports the relevant wire-routing compatibility, especially for the front mech cable routing and housing of junction units..

Frame Specification

From the High Level Specification, you will have decided on the frame material and whether you have a particular brand or design in mind. The next level of detail to consider is the frame geometry.

When comparing frames, there are usually a lot of different lengths and angles to consider, some have a direct impact on the responsiveness, comfort and handling of the bike, others are more useful for comparing sizes between manufacturers.

Geometry Parameters Affecting Responsiveness, Comfort & Handling

The geometric parameter that has the most influence over the responsiveness of a bike is Fork Trail, this is the horizontal distance between the contact point of the tyre with the ground and a line through the centre of the head tube of the frame (as illustrated in the adjacent diagram).

A bike with a smaller fork trail will be more responsive than a bike with a longer fork trail.

Responsiveness is good for fast-manoeuvring, such as on a race bike, but can feel less stable and twitchier, so less desirable on a touring bike.

Unfortunately, not many manufacturers provide this measurement. The most relevant measure that is typically provided is the head tube angle. A steeper (larger) head tube angle generally equates to less fork trail and therefore more responsiveness. A slacker (lower) head tube angle typically leads to a more stable bike.

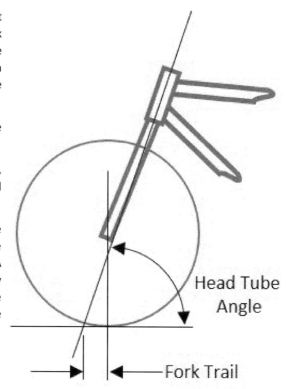

Other key measurements to consider that affect comfort and handling are:

Wheelbase (distance between wheel axles)
A longer wheelbase will be more stable, a shorter wheelbase will be more responsive.

Seat Tube Angle
A steeper seat tube shifts the rider's weight forward, which increases responsiveness.

Chain-Stay Length
Shorter chain-stays imply a shorter wheelbase and thus more responsiveness.

Head Tube Length
With a short head tube, the rider will be lower on the bike and therefore more aerodynamic; but such a riding position may lead to back and neck discomfort. Touring bikes therefore have taller head tubes than time-trial bikes.

The diagram below illustrates the typical parameters for different styles of road bike.

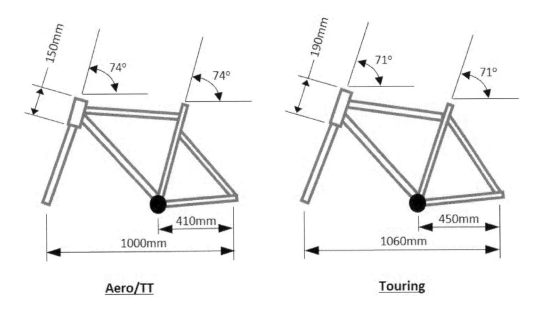

Aero/TT   **Touring**

Comparing Frame Size from Different Manufacturers

Typically, frame sizes are quoted as the length of the seat tube (in cm for road bikes and inches for hybrid and MTB). However the seat tube length can be quite different for two bikes of the same actual size depending on the top tube angle. There is also no standard for this measurement, some manufacturers measure to the very end of the seat tube, whilst others measure to the intersection of the top tube with the seat tube.

A more representative method of comparing frame sizes is to use "stack" and "reach" measures, which are usually provided from manufacturers. Stack is measured vertically from the centre of the bottom bracket to the centre of the top of the head tube. Reach is measured horizontally from the centre of the bottom bracket to the centre of the top of the head tube; as illustrated.

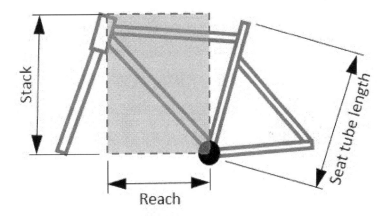

In order to determine the correct stack and reach for yourself, there are a number of calculators available to help you with ball-park values, but ideally you will need to test-ride several bikes to gauge what is correct for you (or go for a bike fit). Using the measures of stack and reach enable you to translate sizes across different manufacturers if you can't test-ride the exact bike of your choice.

Note also that you will still be able to make adjustments to saddle position, stem length and handlebar size but you need to make sure the frame is close to ideal initially.

Frame Design Features

Your choice of frameset may also be driven by particular design features, such as:

- Integral suspension features (e.g. Specialized's Future Shock or Pinarello's K8)
- Fully-concealed cables – whereby the gear and brake cables/hoses are routed within the handlebars, stem and headtube (see photo below).

Headset, Bottom Bracket & Seatpost Interfaces

Another minefield to navigate is the range of different interfaces used for headsets, bottom brackets and seatposts.

Head Tube

Head tubes are either straight or tapered and have a variety of formats for the headset bearing fitment (headset bearings will be covered in a later chapter). At this point in the specification process, you just need to check that the head tube of the frame will be compatible with the steerer tube on the forks – check the dimension at top and bottom of both head tube and steerer.

Tapered Head Tube & Steerer

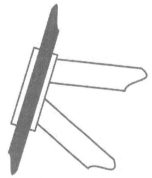

Straight Head Tube & Steerer

If you buy the frame and forks together as a frameset, then this should not present an issue.

Bottom Bracket

Bottom brackets (BB) fall into two categories:

1) Threaded – the frame has internal threads for the bearings to screw into;
2) Press-fit – the frame does not have a thread, a press-tool is used to push the bearings/cups into the frame.

The specific details for BB bearings are covered in a later chapter, this section summarises the differences between the two categories.

BB Type	Advantages	Disadvantages
Threaded	Simple tools required to assemble / remove. Generally no issues once fitted. Wide choice of cranks and bearings.	Most threaded BB formats are for 24mm axles and a frame BB width between 68-73mm – limiting the frames's strength and stiffness compared to Press-fit BBs.
Press-fit	Allows bigger and wider BBs and thus stiffer frames and improved tyre clearance, as well as larger diameter crank axles for increased stiffness and reduced weight. Weight saving for carbon frames where the bearing cups press directly into carbon (no metal inserts in the frame).	Press tool required to fit. Prone to creaking if not manufactured within very tight tolerances nor assembled correctly.

Seatpost Tube Diameter

Take note of the internal diameter of the frame's seat tube and match with the seatpost, usual diameters include:

- 25.4mm (found on some hybrid bikes and BMX)
- 27.2mm
- 30.9mm
- 31.6mm
- 34.9mm

A wider diameter seatpost will tend to be stiffer/stronger, i.e. for MTB use. A narrower seatpost will be more compliant, i.e. good for touring bikes.

Note that bikes with aero-profiled tubing will require a specific aero-profile seatpost.

Frameset Detailed Specification

Before proceeding, please write down your answers for the following questions:

1) What are your specific requirements for mounting points or cable routing for the frame?
2) What is your preferred frame geometry?
3) What is your required Stack and Reach dimensions?
4) Have you checked compatibility between the frame head tube and fork steerer diameters?
5) Do you have a specific requirement for the type of bottom bracket on the frame?
6) Do you have a specific requirement for the seatpost diameter of the frame?

Frame and Forks – Additional Considerations for MTB

For mountain bikes, there are additional considerations, especially regarding the suspension components as illustrated in the following decision chart.

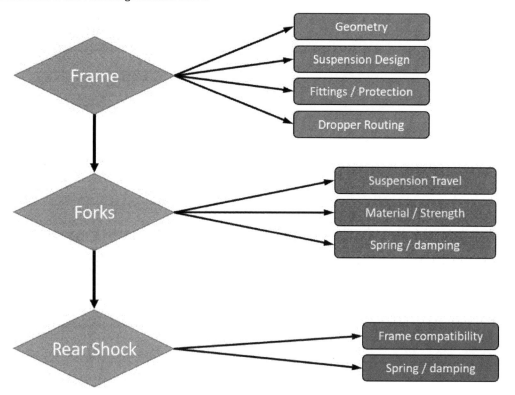

Mountain Bike Frames

From the High Level Specification, you will have considered:

- Whether you require a hardtail or a full suspension MTB;
- Frame material;
- Target cost.

Additional lower-level considerations for MTB frames to guide you to a short-list include:

1) Frame Geometry
2) Suspension design and travel;
3) Frame fittings and protection;
4) Routing for a dropper seatpost.

Mountain Bike Frames

Frame Geometry

All the generic geometric features also apply to mountain bike frames, but there are additional parameters to consider that are specific to mountain bikes.

Mountain bikes typically have shallower head tube angles and longer wheelbases than road bikes to help with stability over rough terrain, with downhill bikes having the most extreme of these dimensions, as illustrated below. Note also that longer-travel forks (e.g. 200mm for a downhill bike) will raise the stack height compared to a cross-country bike with 120mm travel.

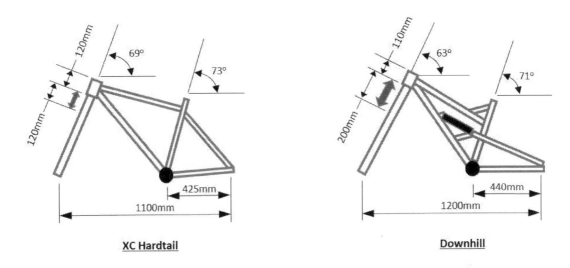

XC Hardtail   Downhill

Two other important frame measurements to consider are:

- Stand-over height, (typically measured at the mid-point of the top tube), which could result in lots of pain and discomfort if it greater than your inside leg measurement!

- BB Drop, which determines the ground-clearance of the crank, chainring and pedals - a higher BB gives more clearance but raises the overall centre of gravity of the bike, which reduces stability.

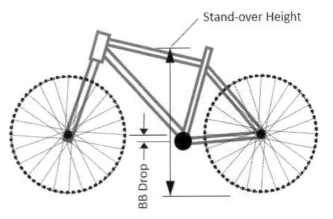

Suspension Design

There are a number of different configurations of rear suspension, each with different strengths and weaknesses. The diagram below illustrates four common designs.

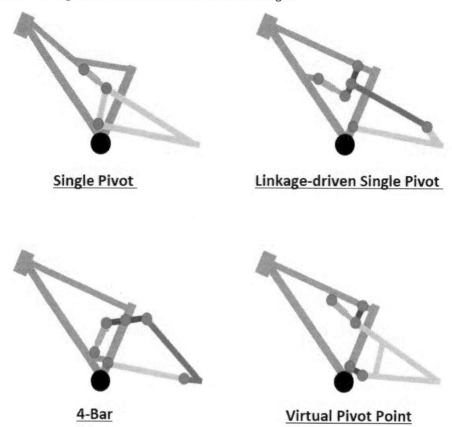

The key issues facing bike designers regarding rear suspension are:

Pedal Bob: whereby the suspension travels up and down in response to pedalling action;

Brake Squat/Jack: whereby the suspension travels either up or down when braking;

Chain Length: whereby the chain length changes as the suspension travels through its range.

The main pros and cons of each design are summarised as follows:

Design	Pros	Cons
Single Pivot	Simplicity and lower cost Good durability	Brake squat Chain length extension
Linkage Driven	Able to tune spring/damping motion	Pedal bob Brake squat
4-Bar	Good control when braking	Pedal bob Lots of moving parts requiring maintenance
Virtual Pivot Point	Good control for both braking and pedalling Strength due to short links and rigid rear triangle	Increased weight Complex set up and tuning

Suspension Travel

Mountain bike frame geometries are based around a specific fork length, which is determined by the amount of suspension travel of the fork. If you fit a longer fork, then the head tube angle will become slacker, slowing down the handling of the bike and also increasing the load on the join between the head tube and down tube. If you fit a shorter fork than intended, the handling will become more aggressive.

For full-suspension bikes, the general rule is to match the travel of the rear suspension with that of the front fork (i.e. use a fork with 160mm travel with a frame that has 160mm travel).

Frame Fittings and Protection

For more aggressive riding, you may also wish to include the following:

- Chain Guides;
- Bash Guards;
- Protection Covers.

Chain Guides are used to minimise occurrences of dropping the chain and are available in a number of formats and mounting styles. Chain guides can be mounted as follows:

1) Using ISCG (International Standard for Chain Guide) mounts, which are threaded tabs integral to the frame around the bottom bracket. There are two different formats: ISCG05, which has a BCD of 73mm, and ISCGold, which has a BCD of 59.4mm.
2) Bottom bracket mounted, sandwiched between the bearing cup and the frame.
3) Seat tube mounted, similar to a front mech.

Chain guides are available as upper guide only (used mainly for 1x drivetrains in place of a front mech), bottom guide only (for 2x drivetrains), bottom roller (to extend chain wrap around the chain ring) or a combination of these into a single unit.

Bash Guards also attach at the bottom bracket and enclose the lower portion of the chain ring so as to protect the chain ring from damage when riding over rough terrain.

Protection Covers are usually self-adhesive and can be added to the frame (e.g. chain-stays) to offer protection against damage – especially important for carbon frames as deep scratches or wear-marks can weaken the frame.

Dropper Seatpost Cable/Hose Routing

There are two formats of routing for dropper seatposts, as illustrated below.

1) Internal routing, also termed "stealth routing", requires an access hole in the frame for the cable/hose to exit near the bottom bracket.
2) External routing, with the cable/hose running down the outside of the seatpost in a loop to allow for the travel of the saddle. This does not require any specific frame features for fitment.

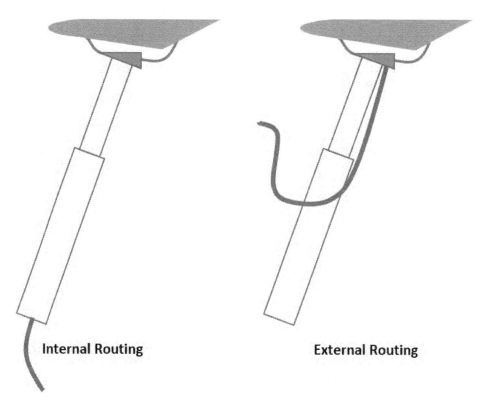

Internal Routing   External Routing

Mountain bike frames will typically specify if they are intended for internal dropper routing or not.

Note that some dropper seatposts are available with the cable/hose attaching to the lower part of the seatpost rather than by the saddle, avoiding the loop in cable/hose.

Mountain Bike Forks

From the High Level Specification, you will have considered:

- Suspension Travel;
- Intended use and therefore strength requirements;
- Budget – i.e. the price-ranking in the model range.

From the above, you may well already be constrained to a single product (or comparable products from different manufacturers). The following section will cover the specification features of suspension forks in more detail and cover:

- Detailed anatomy of forks and the differences relating to strength and weight;
- Springs and damping;
- Axles and axle clamping.

Fork Anatomy

Mountain bike forks comprise the following components, as shown in the diagram below:

Steerer Tube: connects the fork to the frame via the headset.

Stanchions: typically the upper leg and inner sliding component of the telescopic suspension.

Crown: connects the steerer tube to the stanchions. Downhill forks often have a double-crown structure as shown.

Lower leg: the main lower component of the fork onto which the wheel mounts.

Controls: usually mounted on the crown (but sometimes also underneath the lower legs), these control the spring and damping action of the fork.

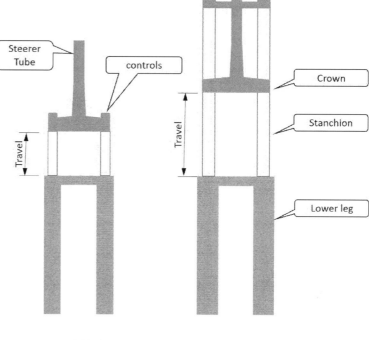

Trail Fork   Downhill Fork

Forks also vary in **strength and materials** depending on the price and their intended use:

Light-duty forks, for cross country and light trail use, will have slimmer stanchions (e.g. 28-32mm) and corresponding lower legs; travel will be in the range of 100-120mm. Stanchions will typically be aluminium alloy, lower legs on premium forks will be made from magnesium with a 1-piece carbon fibre crown/steerer. Weight will be around 1.4kg for premium forks, whilst budget forks will be around 2kg.

Mid-duty forks for trail and enduro-style riding will have wider stanchions (e.g. 35mm), travel will be in the range of 120-170mm. Stanchions, crown and steerer will typically be aluminium alloy, lower legs on premium forks will be made from magnesium. Weight will be around 2kg.

Heavy-duty forks for downhill riding will also have wider stanchions (up to 40mm), travel will be in the range of 170-210mm. Stanchions, crowns and steerer will typically be aluminium alloy, lower legs on premium forks will be made from magnesium. Weight will be around 2.5kg.

Many forks are also adjustable regarding travel, i.e. you can add inserts within the fork's suspension mechanism to reduce the travel.

Springs and Damping

There are typically three aspects to springs and damping:

1) Spring type and rate;
2) Compression damping and lock-out;
3) Rebound damping.

Spring Type and Rate

There are two types of spring used; traditional coil springs and air springs. Coil springs are used on either entry-level forks, whereby basic springs are used to keep the cost low, or on downhill forks where weight is less of an issue and durability is paramount. Air springs are lighter; with most forks having a single air spring in one of the legs, with the damping mechanism in the other leg.

Coil-sprung forks usually have a pre-load adjuster to setup for the required rider's weight. Adjusting the spring-rate of coil springs typically involves dismantling the fork and swapping the coil spring for one of a different rate.

The primary method of adjusting air springs is by altering the air pressure within the spring by means of attaching a pump to the valve on the controls on the fork crown. Further adjustments to the profile of the spring-rate can be made by inserting spacers within the mechanism in the fork. Manufacturers typically list the air pressure required based on the rider's weight.

Compression Damping and Lock-Out

Entry-level forks usually have the ability to lock-out the suspension on the fork, which allows for more efficient riding, for example when on steady ascents or road sections. More advanced forks offer a number of settings for the degree of damping, via a control dial on the crown or via a remote control on the handlebars. Premium forks have further adjustability with separate controls for low-speed damping (i.e. pedalling) and high-speed damping (e.g. impact).

Rebound Damping

Rebound damping controls how "bouncy" the fork feels over a bump, minimal rebound damping will mean the fork will extend quickly, whereas a lot of damping will mean a slow response. Most forks have a control dial to tune the setting as you require – often at the base of one of the legs.

Rear Shocks

As described above, the travel of the rear suspension should align with the fork travel and many frames are sold together with the rear shock, so you may not need to specify the rear shock separately. However you may be considering buying a rear shock either as part of a bike build or as an upgrade. The key features to consider for rear shocks are:

- Frame mounting / compatibility;
- Spring and damping specification.

Frame Mounting / Compatibility
The basic anatomy of a rear shock is illustrated below.

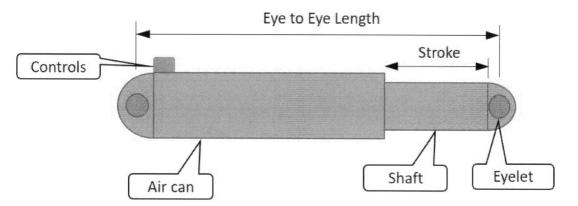

To ensure compatibility, check the following features:

- **Eye-to-eye length** – match the shock to the frame specification.

- **Stroke**, this is the total travel of the shock, not the total suspension travel of the frame – the difference due to the leverage of the suspension design.

- **Shock mounting hardware** (bolts, bushes, etc.) – these are not usually supplied with the rear shock and will need to match both the shock and the frame in terms of internal/external diameter and length. If possible match the make of the mounting hardware to the make of the shock.
  Also available are offset bushes that enable small changes to fitment and tuning.

- **Frame clearance** – some shocks have an external reservoir tank, also there can be multiple controls in different locations on the shock – make sure there is clearance to fit the shock to the frame and also have access to all the controls.

Springs and Damping

For the spring component of a rear shock, as per front forks, there are two main choices:

1) **Coil Spring** – used on entry level bikes or downhill bikes
2) **Air Spring** – found on most full suspension bikes

Coil springs are much cheaper than air springs but add significant weight (e.g. extra 400g). Other than their use on entry-level bikes (to keep the cost low), they are still extensively used for heavier-duty mountain bikes (e.g. downhill) where weight is less of an issue; one major benefit for coil springs is they offer a smoother action with less stiction than an air spring.

Adjusting the rate of a coil spring will require a swap of springs, whereas air shocks can be adjusted by virtue of higher or lower air pressure.

If you are intent on a coil spring but want to reduce the weight then higher grade steel and titanium springs are available.

In contrast, **air springs** are lighter but more expensive due to their complexity – specifically the technology needed to provide durable sealing for the high air pressures utilised. Their use extends across the price and usage range of most mountain bikes, with newer designs becoming more common on downhill bikes.

For **damping**, similar to front forks, rear shocks have controls for both compression and rebound damping. The following features and controls are available for consideration (though not necessarily all on one unit).

- High-speed compression damping (big bumps, jumps, etc.);
- Low-speed compression damping (small bumps, uneven paths, etc.);
- Suspension lock-out (to improve pedalling efficiency when climbing or on roads);
- Platform damping (minimises effects of pedal bob);
- Rebound damping;
- Additional "piggy back" reservoirs (reduces overheating, additional compression damping control);
- Pre-load spring adjustment (for coil springs);
- Air pressure valve (for air springs);
- Remote control (handlebar mounted control for suspension lock-out).

MTB Frameset Detailed Specification

Before proceeding, please write down your answers for the following questions:

1) What is your fork specification (material, damping features, and axle standard)?
2) What is your preferred MTB frame suspension design type?
3) What are your specific requirements for mounting points (e.g. chain guides) or seatpost cable routing for the frame?
4) What size/standard rear shock do you need (including mounting hardware)?
5) What is your rear shock specification (spring and damping features)?
6) Do you have a specific requirement for the seatpost diameter of the frame (especially if you plan to reuse a dropper seatpost)?

Brakes

From the High Level Design you will have already decided:

- Type of brakes (rim, disc, hub or coaster);
- Whether to use cable-operated or hydraulic brakes.

The next level of detail encompasses the following stages of specification:

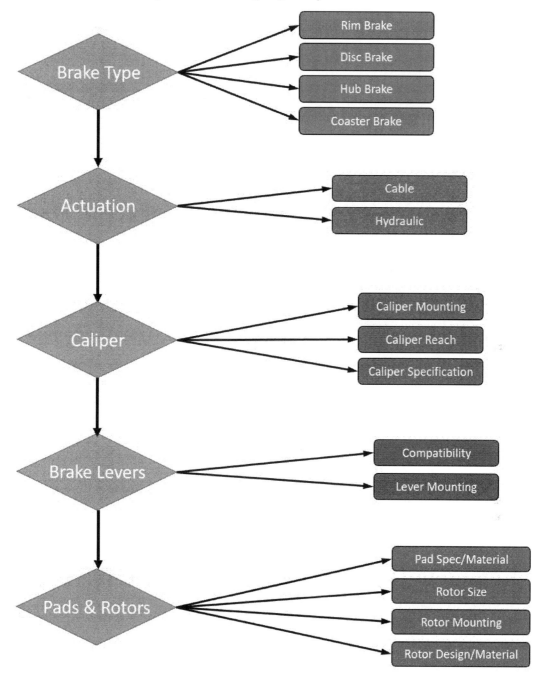

The following sections of this chapter will focus on rim and disc brakes, covering in turn: calipers, levers, brake pads/blocks and rotors.

For hub brakes, only the section on brake levers will be of relevance. For coaster brakes, none of this chapter will be relevant (unless you fit additional rim or disc brakes to the bike).

Brake Calipers

Calipers for Rim Brakes

For cable-operated rim brakes, there are five distinct types of brakes, with different mounting requirements regarding the frame and forks, as illustrated below.

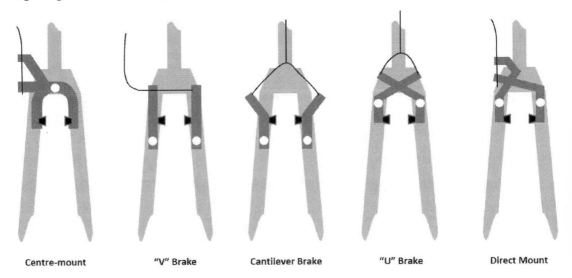

| Centre-mount | "V" Brake | Cantilever Brake | "U" Brake | Direct Mount |

Centre-mount brakes require a single drilled hole in the middle of the fork crown or frame tube. The brake caliper has a bolt which inserts into the hole with a nut attached on the other side. This format of caliper is typically found on road bikes. This type of brake is not suitable for use with suspension forks.

V-Brakes require threaded bosses on the fork legs and rear-stays, which are located lower than the wheel rim. These brakes are used on budget mountain and hybrid bikes and can be used with front suspension.

Cantilever Brakes use the same mounting as V-Brakes but require a cable mount on the frame so will not work with front suspension.

U-Brakes also require threaded bosses on fork legs and seat-stays, but located above the wheel rim. This format of brake is typically used on BMX bikes as the cable run is less obtrusive than the other formats.

Direct Mount brakes are a newer development for road bikes and offer greater stiffness and improved aerodynamics than centre-mount brakes. However the frame and forks need corresponding mounting bosses. For the rear brake, mount points can be either on the seat-stays or under the bottom bracket.

Centre-mount Caliper Reach

If you are going to use centre-mount calipers, then check the frame specification regarding caliper reach (distance from mounting hole to wheel rim).

Frames and forks intended for wider tyres or with mudguard clearance (e.g. gravel or winter bike) may have a reach dimension requiring a longer-reach caliper than those found in typical groupsets, which you would have to purchase separately (e.g. standard reach is around 49mm, longer-reach will be around 57mm).

Centre-mount Rim Brake Caliper Specification

If you are going to buy a whole groupset, this will most likely determine the caliper choice, but there may be options available (e.g. centre-mount or direct mount) – but also check the reach measurement, as per above.

If you are sourcing the calipers separately then there are three options:

1) Hydraulic rim brakes, very limited choice for either full hydraulic systems (e.g. SRAM) or hybrid systems with a control unit with a cable input and hydraulic output to the caliper (e.g. Magura);
2) Single pivot caliper (older brakes or entry-level bikes);
3) Dual pivot caliper (on most modern road bikes).

The difference between single pivot and dual pivot is illustrated in the adjacent diagram. Single-pivot calipers utilise the mounting bolt as the pivot for both arms, dual pivot calipers have pivot locations integral to the caliper mechanism (still with a single bolt to attach to the bike). Dual-pivot calipers have more leverage and stiffer arms than single-pivot calipers, therefore provide better braking performance.

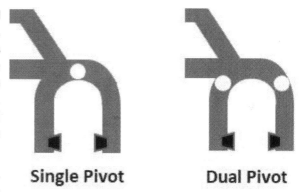

Single Pivot   **Dual Pivot**

Note that direct-mount calipers are also dual-pivot, with the mounting bolts forming the pivot points.

Caliper Nut Length

Note, you may need to buy a longer-reach (or shorter) nut to attach the caliper to the frame and/or forks, especially for deep fork crowns and thicker frame tubes.

Some calipers are provided with several nuts of different lengths to overcome this potential issue.

Some frame and fork specifications may list specific requirements for longer-reach nuts

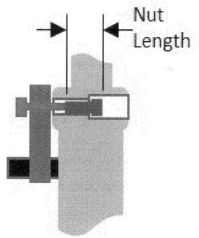

Calipers for Disc Brakes

There are several methods for mounting disc brakes, as illustrated below.

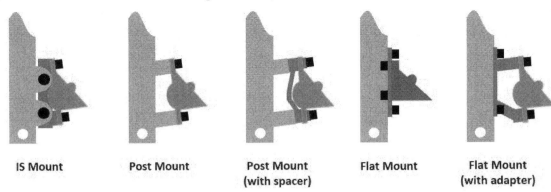

| IS Mount | Post Mount | Post Mount
(with spacer) | Flat Mount | Flat Mount
(with adapter) |

IS Mount (International Standard) uses a bracket in between the caliper and frame/fork. Different brackets can be used to cater for different diameter rotors.

In a **Post Mount** installation, the caliper bolts directly to the frame/fork. This will only function with the minimal rotor diameter as specified with the frame/forks.

For Post Mount calipers with larger rotors, a **spacer** is sandwiched between the caliper and the frame/fork; note that the spacer is thicker on the outer edge to align with the curvature of the rotor – this necessitates the use of double-conical washers as there is an angle formed between the head of the bolt and the caliper, longer bolts are also required.

Note: the same design of caliper will fit with each of the above mounting methods.

Flat Mount is a newer (sleeker) standard for road bikes, whereby the caliper has threaded holes. This is a different caliper standard from the other three methods and cannot be fitted to other mounting systems. The frameset needs to align with this standard as the rear caliper bolts pass through holes in the chain-stay. The front caliper is bolted to a flat mounting plate, which in turn is bolted to the fork.

Flat-mount calipers will only work with 140mm or 160mm diameter rotors. For the front caliper, the mounting plate is inverted to switch between the rotor sizes; the rear requires a spacer to be used for a 160mm rotor.

Adapter brackets are available to fit "standard" (non-flat-mount) calipers to framesets with mounting holes for flat-mount calipers.

Disc Brake Caliper Specification

For cable-operated calipers, the majority of calipers all work the same way in that one of the pads is fixed in the caliper and the other pad moves when operated (i.e. the rotor is pushed against the fixed pad). More money typically means less weight and/or more durable materials.

For hydraulic calipers, the "standard" caliper has a piston on each side, both of which move simultaneously to push the pads against the rotor. Over and above the standard specification, the following features are available:

- 4-piston - this design has two pistons on each side, enabling larger pads to be used – this design is typically only used for downhill mountain bikes;
- Cooling fins – some calipers have fins on the body to improve heat dissipation;
- Features to aid the bleed procedure.

If you are going to use hydraulic brakes, then I would recommend you purchase the lever/shifter and caliper as a unit to ensure compatibility. Lever and caliper assemblies, when purchased as a unit are typically supplied assembled to the hose and bled air-free. If your frame/fork has internal routing, you will have to undo the hose & re-bleed. Most likely, you will also need to shorten the rear hose and re-bleed the brake.

Note that different hydraulic oils are used by different manufacturers – for example:

- Shimano uses a mineral oil;
- Campagnolo uses a mineral oil;
- SRAM uses DOT brake fluid (automotive).

Note that you cannot mix DOT 5 with DOT 5.1, but DOT 5.1 can be used with DOT 3 & 4

Do not mix any components or tools with different types of the above fluids (e.g. don't use a bleed kit that has had DOT fluid in it for bleeding mineral oil brakes).

Mixing mineral oils across different manufacturers may work but will void your warranty.

Brake Levers

For bikes with **drop handlebars**, you will typically use a combined brake lever with gear shifter unit, as described in the drivetrain section. If you are using bar-end or downtube gear levers, then you could use either a combined brake/gear lever (without connecting a gear cable) or a specific drop handlebar brake lever without gear control. You may also have a requirement for additional secondary brake levers underneath the top section of drop handlebars; levers are available that mount in-line with the brake cable to offer this functionality.

For bikes with **flat handlebars**, the brake lever needs to match the brake caliper – specifically matching the cable-pull ratio for cable-operated brakes (e.g. levers for V-Brakes operate with a different pull-ratio to centre-mount calipers).

For **hydraulic levers for flat handlebars** (e.g. MTB levers), the following features are available:

- Split-clamp – this allows you to remove the brake lever without removing the grip;
- Bite-point adjustment – control over how far the lever moves before the pads touch the rotor;
- Lever-reach – allows the lever to sit closer to the handlebar (e.g. for smaller hands);
- Easier bleed – improved bleed procedure;
- Lever profile – better grip and/or increased leverage.

Brake Lever Mounting

There are a number of options for mounting flat-bar brake and gear levers to consider, as described in the Drivetrain section but repeated here for completeness.

- Separate levers, each with their own clamp – this is usually termed "Bar Mount";
- Levers that share a single handlebar mount – there are various standards, such as:
    - Shimano uses: I-Spec A, I-Spec B, and I-Spec II;
    - SRAM uses MMX (Matchmaker X), which will hold three components (brake, gear & dropper seatpost remote control).

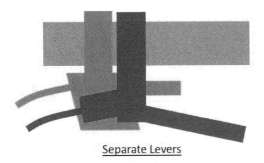

Separate Levers

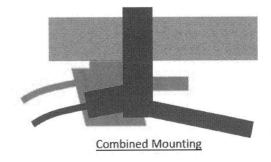

Combined Mounting

Brake Pads and Rotors

Brake pads for rim brakes are usually supplied together with the brake caliper, however you may decide to replace or upgrade the pads either as part of the bike build or during routine maintenance. Note that there are several mounting types, as illustrated below.

Unthreaded post   **Threaded post with nut**   **Bolt**

- **Unthreaded post**: usually for V-Brakes and Cantilever brakes;
- **Threaded post**: usually for MTB and BMX;
- **Bolt**: usually for road bikes.

Each of the above pads are also available as a non-serviceable one-piece moulding or as replaceable pads that insert into a pad housing and are retained with a clip or screw – if ordering separate pads then check the compatibility with the housing and brake caliper.

There is also a range of materials available for rim brake pads:

- **Economy** pads from lower grade rubber compounds;
- **Softer rubber** compounds which cause less rim-wear;
- **High grade rubber** for improved wet weather braking;
- **Carbon-wheel** pads – necessary for using with wheels with carbon braking surfaces.

Note: if you are unhappy with your bike's braking performance (especially in wet weather), then it might be worth considering upgrading the brake pads.

Brake pads for disc brakes are available in over 20 shapes and sizes and must be matched to the caliper – check before ordering. The pads are also typically available in three choices of material:

- **Resin** (also called "Organic"): suitable for most applications and most rotor materials;
- **Metallic** (also called "Sintered"): improved wear, heat resistance and wet weather performance but prone to noise and require stainless steel rotors;
- **Semi-metallic**: a blend of the above, but require stainless steel rotors.

Note also that some pads are available with a choice of either steel or aluminium backing material – aluminium-backed pads are usually more expensive but are lighter and better heat conductors.

Rotors for Disc Brakes

Rotors are available in two different mounting formats, as illustrated below:

1) **6-Bolt**, where the rotor is bolted to the wheel hub;
2) **Center-lock**, where the rotor is mounted on spline with a retaining ring.

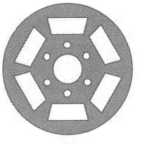

Note: adapters are available to interchange the different rotor types with hubs.

<u>6-Bolt</u>   <u>Center-lock</u>

Rotors are also available in a range of diameters, the most common ones are:

- 140mm
- 160mm
- 180mm
- 203mm

Smaller rotors are lighter and are typically used on road-going bikes, where traction will be limited by the tyre and braking generally less intense than for mountain bikes; the biggest rotors will tend to be used for downhill mountain bikes.

There are also a range of designs and materials available for rotors, key features to note are:

- Entry-level rotors will be made of lower-grade steel and can only be used with resin pads - the rotors are usually stamped with "resin pad only";
- Shimano's "Ice" technology utilises an aluminium rotor (light weight and good heat transfer) sandwiched with stainless steel faces (durability);
- Floating Disc rotors, usually have an aluminium centre with a stainless steel outer constructed to allow the outer to expand without cracking the inner;
- SRAM's Centerline rotors, which have a pattern optimised to reduce vibration and hence braking noise.

<u>Brakes Detailed Specification</u>

Before proceeding, please write down your answers for the following questions:

1) Which type of caliper mounting system will you need?
2) Do you need any adapters, spacers or longer bolts to mount the calipers?
3) Do you have any specification requirements for the calipers (make, fluid type, cooling features)?
4) Which brake lever mounting system will you need?
5) Will you procure brake pads separately, if so what is the specification?
6) For disc brakes, what is the mounting type, diameter and material for the rotors?

Handlebars and Stem

This chapter will take you through the specification detail for the handlebars, stem, bar tape/grips and headset spacers, as illustrated by the decision chart below.

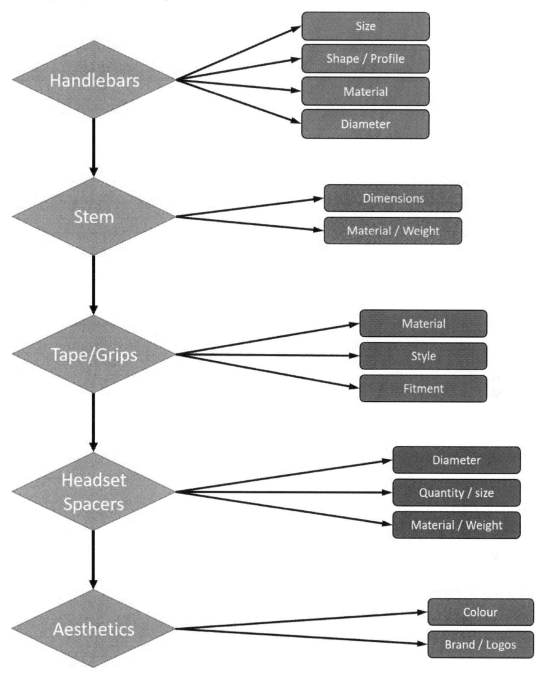

Handlebars

Handlebars fall into three main categories: drop handlebars, flat bars (including MTB riser bars) and aerobars.

Drop Handlebars

There are three principal measurements regarding drop handlebars, as illustrated in the adjacent diagrams.

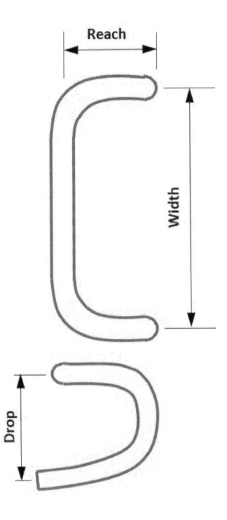

- **Reach** is the horizontal measurement from the centre of the flat bar to the forward-most point of the bars;
- **Width** is usually measured between the centre of the ends of the bars (but some manufacturers measure from the edge of the bars – check before buying);
- **Drop** is the vertical measurement from the centre of the flat bar to the centre of the end of the handlebars.

It is important to select the correct size of handlebars with respect to your body size, the frame size and stem length – it may even be worth fitting old, cheap or borrowed handlebars initially and then going for a bike-fit before ordering the final set.

As a guideline, the following information may help and inform you regarding the choice of bars available.

A common method of determining **handlebar width** is to match the width to the distance between your acromioclavicular (AC) joints – the knobbly bones on the top of your shoulders. But you may also have a preference for narrow bars (e.g. for group riding) or wider bars (e.g. more leverage on a gravel bike).

Handlebar reach will depend on frame size, stem length, your body proportions and your flexibility. Shorter reach bars will typically measure 70mm, through to longer reach bars measuring up to 90mm. (Note, this is a much smaller range than is available with stems.)

Handlebar drop affects the difference in the riding positions between "on the hoods" and "on the drops". The current trend for general riding is to use "compact" bars which have a smaller drop, which is around 120mm, compared to traditional handlebars with drops up to 145mm.

Handlebars are also available in a variety of different shapes and profiles, including:

- Aero-section tubing;
- Flared profile, with a greater width at the bar ends than by the shifters;
- Different curve shapes - with associated ergonomic claims

Drop Handlebars with Integrated Stems

If you are certain of the dimensions of your handlebars, as well as the stem length and handlebar rotational orientation, you can achieve further weight savings and improved aerodynamics with a one-piece handlebar-stem - as illustrated.

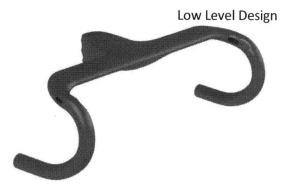

Integrated units also enable fully concealed cable routing when combined with a suitable frameset and headset arrangement – but the tortuous routing may not be suitable for cable operation, and therefore require hydraulic brakes and electronic gear shifting.

Note however that there is no possible adjustment of the overall handlebar-stem reach with this component, therefore it is not recommended unless you are absolutely clear of your needs (and you can source a set to match your exact measurements).

Flat Handlebars

There are four measurements that apply to flat handlebars, as illustrated below.

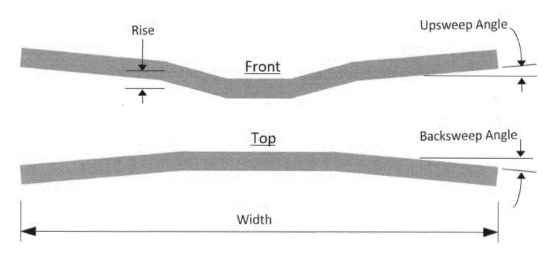

- **Width** is measured from the centres of the bar ends;
- **Rise** is the vertical distance from the centre of the middle of the bars to the centre of the bars after the transition bend;
- **Upsweep** angle is in the vertical plane;
- **Backsweep** angle is in the horizontal plane.

Handlebar width will depend on the intended use for the bike and personal preference. Narrow bars (600mm) will suit a more responsive bike (e.g. cross-country or hybrid use), whereas wide bars (800mm or wider) will provide greater leverage and control (e.g. downhill bikes). Many handlebars have markings on the ends of the bars in 10mm intervals so that you can cut them to a narrower size if preferred. The current trend for mountain bikes is towards wider bars with a shorter stem.

Rise is also a matter of personal preference and will also depend on rider height and the stack height of the bike. Flat bars will have zero rise, whereas a higher-rise handlebar will have a stack of 40mm.

For riser bars (rise greater than zero), **upsweep** will typically be around 5° and **back-sweep** will be in the range of 6°-9°. Flat bars (zero rise) will have a sweep angle in just one plane, which will typically be in the range 5°-9°.

Aero / Tri Bars

There are three options to consider for aerobars, as described below.

Clip-on Extensions - Can be used with conventional drop handlebars (gears and brakes remain on drop handlebars) - easily fitted and removed. - Can also be used with bull-horn base bars (see below) - bar-end gear shifters are typically fitted to these extensions.	
Bull-horn Base Bars - These are fitted instead of drop handlebars and are used in conjunction with clip-on extensions. - Brake levers are typically fitted to the ends of the base bars.	
Integrated Aero Bars - These are typically premium-priced components, constructed from carbon fibre with limited (or zero) adjustability of the position of the extensions.	

Further details that you will need to consider include (test rides recommended before buying):

- cable/wire routing for both gears and brakes;
- width of base bars;
- height of extensions and arm-rests above handlebars;
- distance between extensions;
- profile of extension bars (straight, single bend, double bend).

Handlebar Material

There are two mainstream materials used for handlebars (steel and titanium are also used, but very niche).

1) **Aluminium** – reasonably light and strong, whilst being affordable. Higher grades of aluminium alloys (e.g. 7000-series) are also available at a premium to optimise the balance of strength and weight.

2) **Carbon fibre** – stronger and lighter than aluminium with a higher price-tag, and will help dampen road vibrations. A word of caution though is that any damage to the bike will usually involve the handlebars; carbon fibre is susceptible to impact damage without visible signs and can fail dramatically if damaged.

Handlebar Diameter

There are two distinct diameter measurements for handlebars – as illustrated below:

1) The tube diameter – for mounting levers, shifters and grips;
2) The clamp diameter – which must match with the stem.

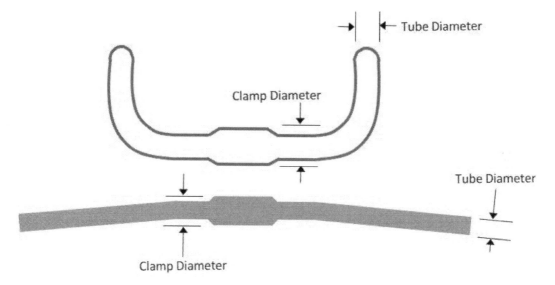

There are various options of handlebars available with different diameters, summarised as follows:

	Drop Handlebars	**Flat/Riser handlebars**
Tube Diameter	23.8mm	22.2mm
Clamp Diameter	25.4mm / 1" (standard ISO size) 26mm (Italian standard) 31.8mm / 1¼" (most popular) 35mm (newer trend)	25.4mm / 1" (standard ISO size) 31.8mm / 1¼" (most popular) 35mm (newer trend)

Stems

The stem not only attaches the handlebars to the bike, but it is also integral to the clamping of the frame, forks and headset; as illustrated below.

Note, this method of component assembly, known as "Threadless Stem", is typical across the majority of modern bikes, replacing the older-style quill stems.

(Mountain bikes with dual-crown forks use the upper crown to clamp the headset; stems are direct-mounted to the upper fork crown rather than the steerer tube.)

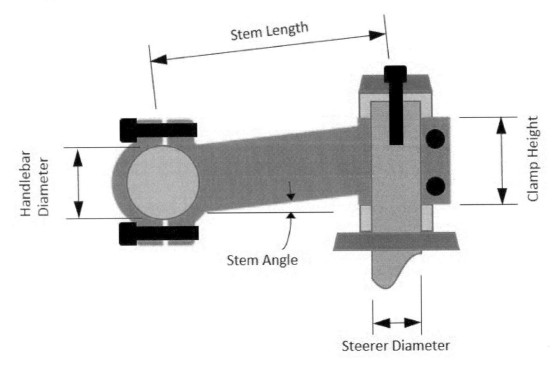

There are a number of parameters that define the stem, these are:

- **Handlebar clamp diameter** – needs to match the handlebars as described previously;
- **Steerer diameter** – needs to match the diameter at the top of the fork steerer tube;
- **Stem length** – determines the fore-aft position of the handlebars;
- **Stem angle** – determines the height of the handlebars relative to the frame;
- **Clamp height** – needs to be taken into account when cutting the steerer tube and selecting headset spacers (explained later in the book).

The most common **steerer diameter** is 28.6mm ($1^1/_8$"), however other sizes exist such as 25.4mm (1") or 38.1mm ($1^1/_2$").

Stem length can vary considerably from very short 30mm stems, usually on mountain bikes, through to long road bike stems of 140mm or longer. The length of the stem affects two factors:

- Riding position on the bike, in conjunction with the reach measurements of both the frame and the handlebars;
- Handling response of the bike – a bike with a shorter stem will respond quicker than with a longer stem but also be "twitchier" and potentially less stable when riding.

The **stem angle** needs to be considered with the stack height of the frame, the rise / drop of the handlebars and the total height of the headset spacers to determine the optimum riding position. Note also that stems can be fitted either way up (flipped), which has a notable impact on the height of the handlebars, as per the diagram below.

The example shown is for a 100mm stem with an angle of 6°, which will change the bar height by 21mm when "flipped".

For a longer stem of 140mm with an angle of 10°, the difference becomes 49mm.

As with handlebars, it may be worth fitting an old, cheap or borrowed stem initially and then going for a bike-fit before ordering the final one.

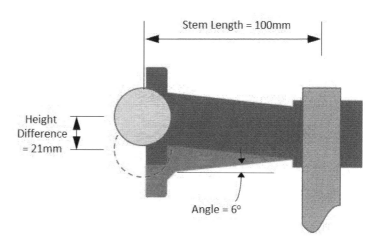

Stem Material and Weight

The vast majority of stems available for both road and mountain bikes are constructed from aluminium alloy. Budget stems will typically use 6061-grade, premium stems will use 2000-series or 7000-series which will offer increased strength or less weight depending on purpose.

Carbon fibre is also used and will offer marginal weight reductions as well as dampen road vibrations but with a much higher price tag. Note also the risk of impact damage.

Bar Tape and Grips

Drop handlebars are typically covered with bar tape, leaving only a short section uncovered in the middle. Flat handlebars typically have grips fitted to both ends.

Aerobars can either be fitted with bar tape or specific aerobar grips with an associated ergonomic profile.

Bar Tape may seem one of the lesser components on a bike but it is the contact interface for your hands and can significantly alter the feel of the bike, so take your time and choose carefully – relative to the rest of the bike a bit more spent on bar tape is a good investment. The parameters to consider are:

- Materials, including:
    - Natural cork, providing good moisture absorption but can wear out quickly;
    - Leather, relatively heavy but reputed for comfort;
    - Synthetic with gel or foam base, lightweight with good durability and comfort;
- Thickness – thicker tape (e.g. 3mm) offers more cushioning and may also suit riders with bigger hands;
- Texture – there are many designs available including smooth, dimpled and perforated;
- Colour – including single colours, two-tone and camouflaged.

In addition to bar tape, you can also add gel or foam cushioning pads under the tape at the main contact points. Also check if the bar tape includes end-plugs, if not you will need to order some!

Also, if you are looking to save weight, note that standard bar tape will weigh around 100g, whilst light-weight tape will be around 50g, including plugs.

Bar Grips are available in three formats, as illustrated below.

Traditional grips are available either with a **flange** on the inside face or without (**flangeless**). It is largely a matter of personal choice, but be aware that a flange can interfere with gear shifters. Adhesive (e.g. hairspray!) is often used to secure the grips to the handlebars but can mean the only way to remove the grip is to cut it off, rendering it non-reusable.

A more modern development is the use of **lock-on** grips, whereby a metal collar is located at each end of the grip and has an Allen bolt that clamps against the handlebars to stop the grip from moving or twisting. Grips can be removed and refitted easily if necessary.

Note that lock-on grips are typically heavier than traditional grips. Also check whether end-plugs are included with the grips.

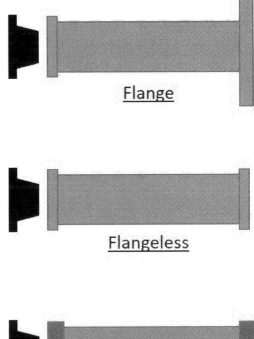

Flange

Flangeless

Lock-on

Other factors to consider with grips include:

- **Grip thickness** – a matter of personal choice and/or hand size;
- **Plain or ergonomic** – plain grips are the same thickness for the whole length of the grip, whereas ergonomic grips have varying thicknesses or moulded profiles over the length of the grip;
- **Material** – grips are typically made from rubber or foam with varying degrees of hardness, some grips are made from two more materials to balance feel and wear;
- **Pattern** – different patterns are used, some more pronounced than others. If possible try the feel of a range of grips before you buy.

Headset Spacers

The role of the headset spacer is to set the vertical position of the stem (and thus the handlebars) relative to the frame. Thicker (or multiple) spacers are used to elevate the stem and thinner (or fewer) spacers to lower the stem. Spacers are also used above the stem where the steerer tube protrudes above the stem as part of the clamping assembly for the headset.

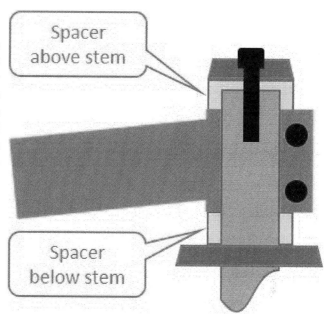

The parameters to consider are:

- **Spacer diameter** – must match steerer (as per stem);
- **Quantity / thickness** – to set the desired stem height and appropriate fit for the headset top cap;
- **Material** – basic spacers are aluminium, but fractional weight savings can be achieved by using carbon fibre or polycarbonate spacers.

Handlebar and Stem Aesthetics

There are lots of choices of colours and styles with the components discussed in this chapter, pay attention to your product selections to ensure they align with your intent – in particular:

- **Handlebars colour and finish**, they are usually black but your chosen item may only be in stock in a different colour.
- **Stems** are available in a wide range of colours, sometimes with the clamp being a different colour than the main body.
- **Tape, grips and headset spacers** are available in a wide range of colours.
- You may also wish to consider matching the **brand** of the handlebars with the stem and also the seatpost (and other components e.g. saddle, crank or wheels).

Handlebars and Stem Detailed Specification

Before proceeding, please write down your answers for the following questions:

1) What is the size of the handlebars?
   a. Road: width, reach, drop
   b. Flat: width, rise, upsweep, backsweep
2) What is the material of the handlebars?
3) What is the length and angle of the stem?
4) Do the stem clamping diameters match the handlebars and steerer?
5) What is the material of the stem?
6) What is the specification of the bar tape/grips (material, fitment method, weight)?
7) What is the size/quantity and material of the headset spacers?
8) Do all of the colours (and logos) align with the intended scheme of the bike?
9) If you plan to use aerobars, have you thoroughly researched your requirements?

Saddle and Seatpost

This chapter will take you through the Low Level Design detail for the saddle, seatpost and seatpost clamp, as illustrated by the decision chart below.

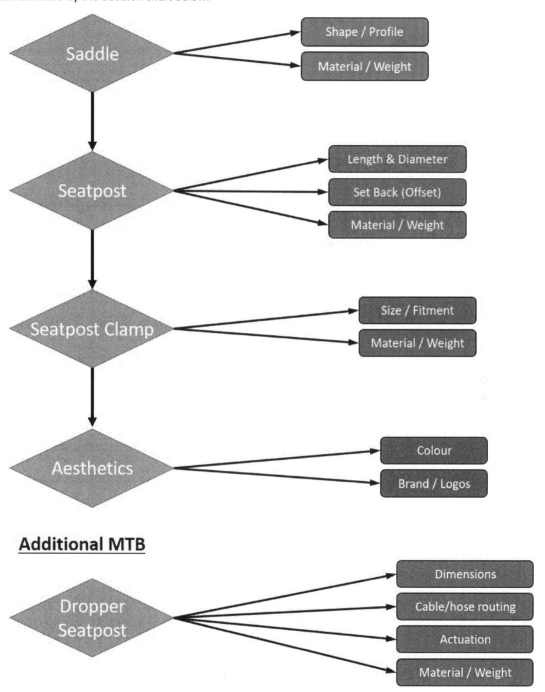

Saddle

The saddle is probably the most important component on the bike – and one that you will get to know intimately! A well-fitting saddle will go unnoticed – an uncomfortable saddle will ruin your ride or even put you off riding ever again!

There are many variables when considering saddles, including shape and construction. The main features of a saddle are:

- **Hull** (or shell), which is the main body of the saddle;
- **Tail**, the rear part of the hull;
- **Nose**, the front of the hull;
- **Rails**, to attach the saddle the seatpost

Tail

Hull

Nose

Rails

(the majority of saddles use a two-rail design, however there is a newer format of a single "I-Beam" design, which is not compatible with two-rail saddles or seatposts).

The shape of the hull will have the biggest impact on fit and will depend on a number of factors including:

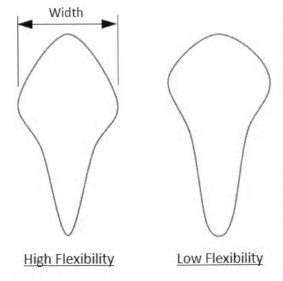

- **The width of your sit bones** (ischial tuberosities). Men have narrower sit bones than women; hence why different saddle shapes. The width of the saddle should be 25-30mm wider than the distance between the sit bones. If your weight isn't supported by the sit bones, then inevitably it will be supported by soft-tissue – causing discomfort or worse.

- **The degree of rotation of your pelvis** (and hence sit bones orientation) when riding, which will depend on your posture, flexibility and riding position (also impacted by other bike-fit factors such as handlebar height and overall reach). A highly rotated pelvis (low flexibility with high forward-lean) will require a saddle with more rearward support. Whereas a person with higher flexibility (or less forward-lean) will suit a saddle with more central support, as illustrated in the above diagram.

- **Padding on the saddle** can help with comfort but less than most people think - it won't change the underlying shape; also if you wear padding in your cycling clothes then this will reduce the need for lots of padding on the saddle itself.

- Saddles can also have **cut-outs or channels** along the centre of the hull to relieve pressure from tender areas.

A number of bike shops have saddle-fit facilities (they will measure your sit-bone width and assess your flexibility / riding position) and may even have a money-back-if-you're-not-happy policy. It's worth trying several saddles before making your mind up – and going for a ride in your cycling clothes rather than just sitting stationary on them.

There are also numerous YouTube videos demonstrating how to measure the width of your sit bones and also assess your flexibility.

Saddles for Aero/TT bikes

The riding position on an aero/TT bike is typically lower and shifted further forward than on a road bike fitted with drop handlebars; consequently the pelvis will be rotated further forward - requiring a different profile saddle.

Numerous different designs are available for you to consider - but you may need to try a range of saddles to find one that enables an efficient riding position that you can maintain for the duration of an event.

Note also the UCI regulation 1.3.013, which states that the nose of the saddle must be a minimum of 5cm vertically behind the centre of the bottom bracket - hence why many TT saddles are of a stubby design!

Saddle Materials and Weight

Budget saddles will have nylon hulls and steel rails - as you pay more the materials advance:

- Hulls can be reinforced with carbon fibre or even constructed completely from carbon fibre;
- Rails are available in a range of materials including manganese, titanium and carbon fibre;
- Covering material includes synthetic materials and layers of foam, leather or even none – just the bare hull.

Saddles can also vary considerable regarding weight:

- A traditional leather "comfort" saddle can be over 500g (a sprung one can be over 800g);
- A budget road/MTB saddle will typically weigh 300-350g;
- A premium road saddle will typically weigh around 150g (with the very lightest ones at around 60g).

Seatpost

There are three dimensions to check with a seatpost, as illustrated in the diagram below.

1) **Seatpost Length** – needs to be long enough to set your required saddle height without extending beyond the minimum insertion mark. Conversely, if it's too long it may result in the saddle being too high for you if it bottoms-out in the frame (or it just adds unnecessary weight).

2) **Seatpost Diameter** – needs to match the internal diameter of the frame's seat tube. As discussed in the Frame section, the common diameters are:
   a. 25.4mm (found on some hybrid bikes and BMX);
   b. 27.2mm;
   c. 30.9mm;
   d. 31.6mm;
   e. 34.9mm.

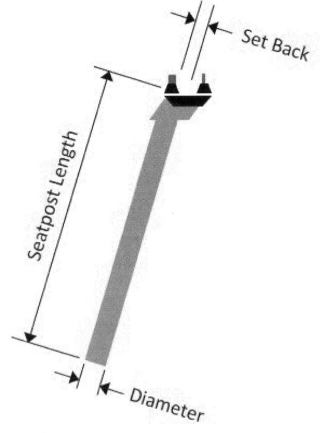

3) **Set Back** – (also termed "offset")
   this is the distance from the centre-line of the post to the middle of the saddle clamp. An increased set-back will move the saddle further back. Seatposts are available with zero set-back (also termed "inline") through to over 30mm. Your actual requirement will depend on the frame geometry and your leg-length. Most seat-rails allow for several millimetres fore-aft adjustment, so pick one with around 10-15mm unless you have good reason otherwise.

Additional notes regarding seatposts:

- If you are converting an existing road bike to an aero/TT bike, then you will need to determine if there are any regulations to comply with (e.g. UCI for seat position and tilt).
- Shims are available to enable you to fit a smaller diameter seatpost to a frame with a larger diameter (but not the other way round!).
- If you are planning to use wired electronic gear control (e.g. Di2 or EPS), then check for seatpost compatibility regarding attaching the battery and routing the wiring.

Seatpost Material and Weight

Lower-cost seatposts are typically made from 6061-grade aluminium and are reasonably light and strong. More expensive alloy seatposts use 7075-grade aluminium to save weight, whilst premium seatposts are made from carbon fibre. Titanium seatposts are available but are typically only used with titanium frames. Comparative weights for non-dropper seatposts are in the region of:

- 6061-grade = 300g;
- 7075-grade = 250g;
- Carbon fibre = 200g.

Another factor to consider is the flex and damping properties of the seatpost with respect to ride comfort; especially for road, hybrid and gravel bikes. A larger diameter, thick-walled alloy seatpost will have minimal flex and damping, whilst a smaller diameter (e.g. 27.2mm) carbon seatpost will flex to a much greater extent and the nature of carbon fibre will also help damp-down road vibrations – both factors contributing to a more comfortable ride.

The exposed length of the seatpost (from the seatpost clamp to the base of saddle) will also affect the flex and damping, so if your saddle-height is set low there may be little noticeable difference between different seatpost materials.

Seatpost Clamp

There are three considerations for seatpost clamps:

1) Diameter;
2) Fastening method;
3) Material / Weight.

The seatpost clamp **diameter** must match the <u>external</u> diameter of the frame's seat tube, as illustrated in the adjacent diagram.

There are five standard diameters of seatpost clamp, namely:

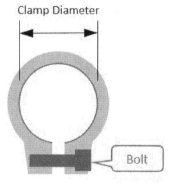

- 28.6mm
- 30mm
- 31.8mm
- 34.9mm
- 36.4mm

Note that there is inconsistency across manufacturers for the relationship between the internal diameter of the seat tube (which dictates the seatpost diameter) and the external diameter (which dictates the seatpost clamp) – some frames are thicker-walled than others, sometimes the clamp area is a different diameter to the rest of the seat tube. Check carefully before you order.

There are three **fastening methods** for seatpost clamps:

1) Separate clamp with one or more Allen bolts;
2) Separate clamp with a quick-release lever;
3) Integral clamp within the frame tube (thus not needed a separate clamp).

Quick-release levers are useful if you frequently adjust the saddle height (e.g. sharing the bike with someone else, needing to lower the saddle for storage or for mountain bikes without a dropper-post). The main disadvantage of quick-release levers is that the clamping force is lower than a clamp with a bolt, so there is potential for the seatpost to slip during a ride.

Regarding **weight and materials,** a typical budget Allen-bolt alloy seatpost clamp weighs around 25g. For those looking to save every possible gram, there are carbon fibre clamps available that weigh less than 10g (but cost several times more than a basic clamp!). A quick-release clamp will weigh more (around 40g).

Saddle, Seatpost and Clamp Aesthetics

As per the previous chapter, there are lots of choices of colours and brands with the components discussed in this chapter, pay attention to your product selections to ensure they align with your intent.

Dropper Seatposts

Dropper seatposts are used on mountain bikes to give the ability to lower and raise the saddle whilst riding and without stopping. The saddle would typically be lowered when tackling a technical descent, so that the rider can move their body behind the saddle, and then raised again for normal riding.

The key parameters for dropper seatposts are:

- Seatpost dimensions;
- Cable/hose routing;
- Actuation method;
- Material / Weight.

The key **dimensions** for dropper seatposts are illustrated in the diagram below.

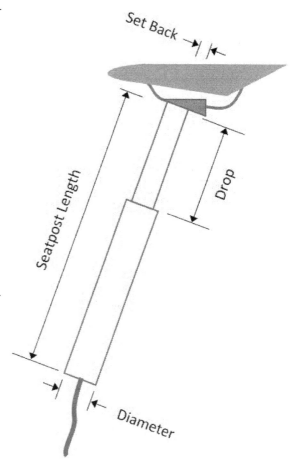

- **Seatpost length** is measured from the seat-rails to the end of the seatpost when the seatpost is fully extended. Choose the length to obtain the correct full saddle height whilst not impacting the minimum insertion length.

- **Drop length** is the maximum distance the saddle will lower when the dropper mechanism is activated. This typically ranges from 75-220mm. Note: shorter riders and/or tall frames may limit the maximum drop you can fit – measure carefully before ordering - otherwise the saddle will be too high, even with the seatpost body fully inserted in the frame.

- **Diameter** needs to match the frame (as per regular seatposts). There are three common sizes available:
  - 30.9mm
  - 31.8mm
  - 34.9mm

- **Set back** (offset) is the distance between the centreline of the post and the saddle clamp. (Most dropper seatposts have zero set-back.)

Cable/hose routing is either internal or external, as described in the Frame and Forks Low Level Design. Internal routing is less obtrusive and less likely to snag on either the rider or obstacles but (depending on the frame) the routing can be more convoluted.

There are four options for seatpost **activation**:

1) **Cable operation**, which is usually straightforward to fit and repair but is prone to dirt;
2) **Hydraulic**, which is more complex to fit (e.g. will need hose shortening and bleeding) but offers smoother action and better resistance to dirt;
3) **Seatpost lever**, whereby you need to take your hand off the handlebar to manually operate the seatpost by means of a lever mounted under the saddle;
4) **Wireless**, whereby the seatpost is actuated electronically from a wireless unit mounted on the handlebars.

For cable and hydraulically-actuated seatposts, you will also need to consider the position of the remote control button or lever on the handlebars. The remote control can be fitted to either the left or right side of the bars and either fitted with the button/lever above the bars or below the bars. Typically, there are two options available to choose between (i.e. swap from left to right to change from above to below).

If you have a 1x11 drivetrain, then usually the seatpost remote control is fitted on the left side – taking the place of the front mech gear lever.

Some remote controls will also support consolidated mounting along with gear shifters and brake levers (e.g. SRAM's MMX).

Button/lever above bars

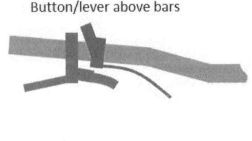

Button/lever below bars

The mainstream **material** for dropper seatposts is aluminium alloy, however more expensive seatposts are available that utilise carbon fibre.

There is a wide variation regarding the **weight** of dropper seatposts, ranging from 400g for carbon-body seatposts up to 700g for heavier alloy seatposts.

Saddle and Seatpost Detailed Specification

Before proceeding, please write down your answers for the following questions:

1) What shape/profile of saddle will you use?
2) What is the material and weight of the saddle?
3) What is the specification of the seatpost (length, diameter & set-back)?
4) What is the material and target weight of the seatpost?
5) Which type of seatpost clamp will you use and what material?
6) (for MTB) What is the travel of the seatpost?
7) (for MTB) What is the actuation method for the seatpost and how will you mount the remote?
8) Do all of the colours (and logos) align with the intended scheme of the bike?

Bearings

There are two sets of bearings that will typically need procuring as part of a bike build, these are the headset and the bottom bracket. The key decision factors are illustrated below.

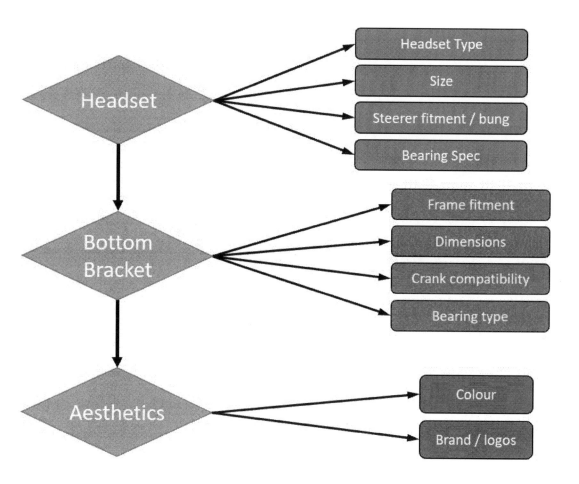

Headset

There are a lot of different types of headsets available, you must choose one that fits both the frame and fork precisely to avoid issues. Some framesets include the headset; in which case you can be certain of compatibility. Many manufacturers list a recommended headset type or at least give sufficient specification details for you to choose one. The rest of the section dives into the detail of headset types and options should you need to reference this level of detail.

Type of Headset

The first parameter to determine is the type of headset you required, there are three common formats in use as illustrated below.

Note, modern bikes will typically use a Threadless Headset (refer to handlebars and stem chapter) with potentially any one of these types of headset, vintage bikes will use a quill stem with a threaded steerer – most likely (but not always) with an external headset.

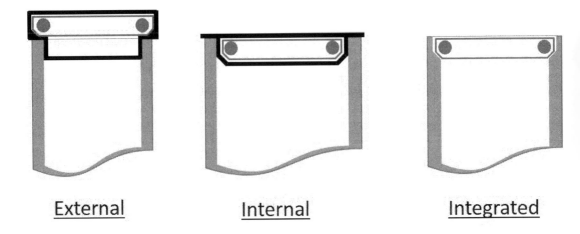

External   Internal   Integrated

External headsets have bearing cups at both ends of the head tube with the bearings housed in the cups externally to the frame. The bearing cups are an interference fit in the frame and require a press-tool for installation.

Internal headsets (also termed "semi-integrated") also have a bearing cup to house the bearings, but typically the frame's head tube is greater in diameter than with external headsets such that the bearings sit within the head tube, offering a more compact installation. As above, a press-tool is required for installation.

Integrated headsets do not have a separate bearing cup, the head tube is machined at each end with an internal chamfer to locate the bearing cartridge. The bearing cartridge is a loose fit in the frame and can be fitted by hand.

Headset Anatomy

The diagram below shows the components within a headset - note that there are no bearing cups for an integrated headset; the bearings sit directly in the frame. Also note, the stem spacers (not shown in the diagram) sit between the dust cap and the top cap.

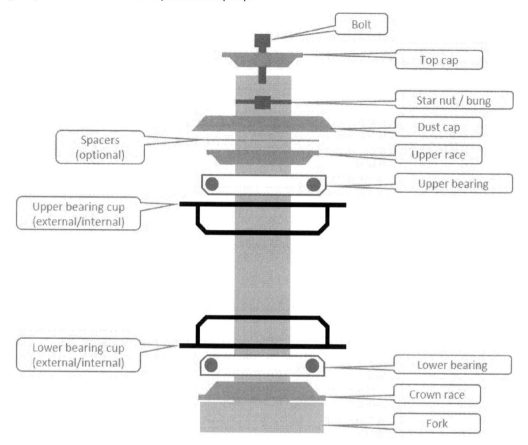

Bolt: clamps the top cap against the stem, spacers, dust cap and upper race to apply a pre-load and eliminate play within the bearings.

Top Cap: sits on top of the stem or headset spacers (must be clear of the top face of the steerer tube).

Star nut: (or compression bung for carbon forks, see later in this section) is fixed inside the steerer tube and secures the bolt.

Dust cap: (also with O-ring seals) keeps dirt out of the top of the headset and is part of the clamping mechanism.

Spacer washers: added (if needed) to ensure clearance between the top cap and the frame's head tube.

Upper race: (also termed compression ring) locates and eliminates play between the upper bearing and the steerer tube.

Bearings: these are typically sealed cartridge bearing units.

Bearing cups: locate the bearings in the frame.

Crown race: locates the lower bearing to the fork crown.

Headset Size

Having determined the headset type, the next set of parameters to consider are the diameters of top and bottom of the head tube and fork steerer. Fortunately, there is a standard to which many manufacturers comply termed the Standardised Headset Identification System (SHIS), which describes the principal dimensions of headsets. The format of the standard is:

Upper		Lower
"AB" "x" / "y"	|	"AB" "x" / "y"

Where "AB" identifies the headset type:

- EC = External headset (external cup)
- ZS = Internal headset (zero stack)
- IS = Integrated headset

"x" identifies the diameter of the head tube, whilst "y" identifies the diameter of the steerer. (Note, these dimensions are rounded as whole numbers, not the accurate measurement itself but they do refer to the accurate measurement within the standard.)

For example, a tapered frame/steerer might require the following headset:

ZS44/28.6 | ZS56/40

Some headsets may also specify the Stack Height, this is the vertical dimension of the headset for components protruding above or below the head tube (this may be listed separately for upper and lower dimensions). In the SHIS standard, this dimension is preceded with an "H".

Practical Notes:

- Headsets may be of mixed types (e.g. Internal lower with External Upper);
- Tapered head tubes may be used with non-tapered steerers if bearings are available to fit the respective upper and lower diameters - and vice versa;
- There are other proprietary headsets that differ from the three types described so far – some comply with SHIS:
  - E.g. Campagnolo Hiddenset – identified as SHIS: IS42 (head tube diameter 41.8mm);
  - Microtech – not described by SHIS;
  - Onepointfive – identified as SHIS EC49 – this is a non-tapered design with a 1.5" steerer.

Special note for full-carbon forks

Full carbon forks (i.e. carbon steerer tube, not alloy) must not use a star nut to secure the headset bolt. A specific compression device (also termed "steerer bung") must be used that clamps to the inside of the steerer tube, as illustrated in the adjacent diagram, without causing damage to the steerer. This needs to be compatible with the internal diameter of the steerer.

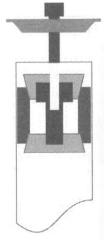

Headset Bearings

Typically, more money buys you higher standards of bearings for the headset with ceramic bearings rolling the smoothest and lasting the longest (but with the highest price-tag!)

Bottom Bracket Bearings

This is another minefield of sizes and standards – and as you are more likely to source the BB bearings separately from the frame, you need to understand which one to buy.

BB Type

From the frame specification, you will have determined whether the BB is threaded or press-fit, however there are multiple options available within these categories.

Threaded Bottom Brackets have bearing cups that screw into the frame from either side. There are two principal options:

1) **Threaded Internal**, whereby the bearings sit within the frame's bottom bracket tube; limiting the diameter of the axle (typically 17mm), which is typically solid. However, some internal BBs are available with larger hollow axles, such as Shimano's Octalink which has a 22mm axle. This type of bottom bracket is found on older and entry-level bikes. The axle is normally supplied as an integral part of the bottom bracket and either has a square taper or splines to secure the crank arms – known as a three-piece crank.

2) **Threaded External**, whereby the bearings sit outboard of the bottom bracket tube, enabling a larger-diameter hollow axle (e.g. 24mm) to be used. The frame's internal diameter is approximately 35mm (depending on thread standard). This type of BB supports Shimano's Hollowtech II, SRAM's GXP and Campagnolo's Ultra-torque.

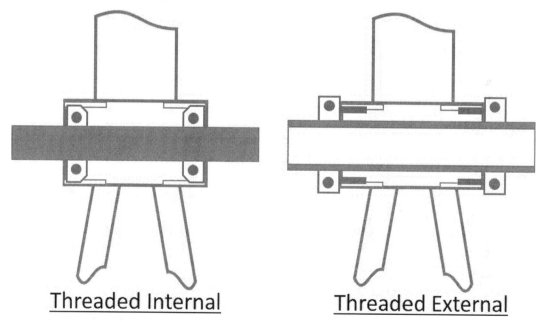

Threaded Internal   Threaded External

Note, the frame BB widths and thread standards also vary as follows:

- English/BSA/ISO Thread – BB width for road bikes is 68mm, for MTB the width is 73mm (spacers can be used to fit a 73mm BB to a 68mm frame (but not vice versa);
- Italian thread – BB width is 70mm (not compatible with English Thread).

Press-fit Bottom Brackets have bearings or cups that are an interference-fit into the frame, and hence require a press-tool for installation. There are also several types available, the two principal designs are illustrated below.

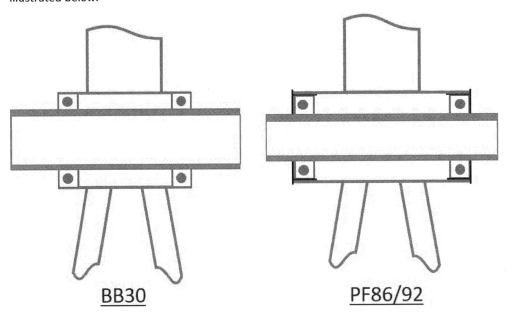

1) **BB30**, which requires the frame to be precision-machined such that the bearings press directly into the frame, this system uses a 30mm axle, and a 42mm frame bore diameter, enabling increased frame stiffness. The BB width is the same as for threaded BBs (68mm for road, 73mm for MTB). Alternative BBs and adapters are available so that a 24mm axle can be used.

2) **PF86/92**, which has a much wider BB width (86mm for road, 92mm for MTB), which enables higher frame stiffness. The frame diameter is 41mm, but the BB design includes bearing cups, which are pressed into the frame (similar to an internal headset). The axle diameter is 24mm, so intended for Hollowtech II, GXP and Ultra-torque.

There are also variants on the above to be aware of:

- **PF30** (PressFit 30), which uses the same 30mm axle size as BB30 but has a 46mm frame diameter and uses bearing cups (similar to an internal headset), so is more tolerant of machining inaccuracies.
- **BB90/95** is Trek's BB system and is similar to PF86/92 but slightly wider (90mm road, 95mm MTB).
- **OSBB** is Specialized's BB system and is very similar to PF30, but with slightly different dimensions.
- **BBright** is Cervelo's proprietary design and is also similar to BB30 but with a wider frame (extra 11mm) to the left-hand side, giving a total width of 79mm, cranks need to be specifically compatible with this system.
- **386EVO**, which is a blend of BB30 and PF86. The frame width is 87mm and the internal diameter is 46mm offering greater frame stiffness than all of the above. Bearing cups are used (like an internal headset) and adapters are available to enable the use of most cranksets, including BB30 and the mainstream 24mm options.
- **T47**, which is essentially a threaded version of PF30.

Bearing Aesthetics

As per previous chapters, there are lots of choices of colours and brands with headsets and bottom brackets in this chapter, pay attention to your product selections to ensure they align with your intent.

Bearings Detailed Specification

Before proceeding, please write down your answers for the following questions:

1) Does your frameset include a headset or do you need to procure one?
2) Does the frame manufacturer specify the headset type/size?
3) (if procuring separately) What is the type and size of the upper and lower headset bearings?
4) (if you have a carbon steerer) What is the specification of the compression device?
5) What is the type and size of the bottom bracket (check compatibility with both frame and crankset)?
   - If Press-fit, how will you install the BB?
6) Do all of the colours (and logos) align with the intended scheme of the bike?

Cables, Hoses and Wires

This chapter will cover the detailed specification of the following components, as illustrated in the decision chart.

- Brake Cables (mechanical) or Hoses (hydraulic);
- Gear Cables (mechanical) or Wires (electronic);
- Seatpost Cable (mechanical) or Hose (hydraulic).

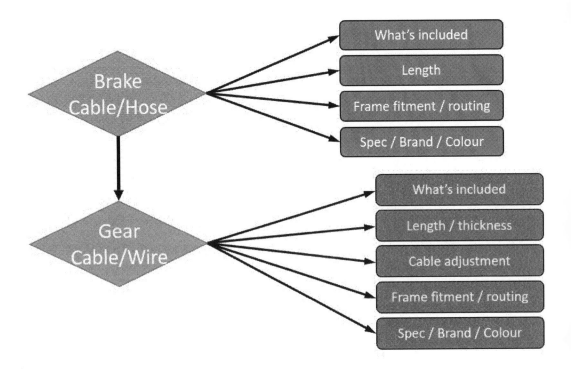

Additional MTB

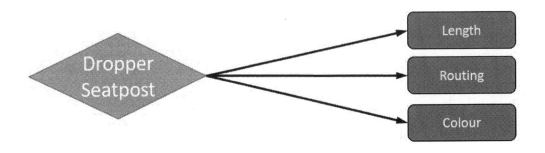

Brake Cables and Hoses

Cable-operated (mechanical) brakes typically have a single cable for each of the front and rear brakes that connects the brake lever to the caliper. You will need to consider the following parameters when selecting the cables:

- Brake cable assembly parts;
- Cable length;
- Frame fitment and routing;
- Cable specification, brand and colour.

Brake cable assemblies consist of a number of separate parts, as illustrated below.

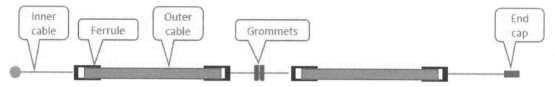

The **inner cable** connects to the brake lever and has a nipple at the end of the cable of varying shapes and sizes depending on application. Road-bike shifter cables use a pear-shaped nipple, whilst flat-bar cables have a cylindrical-shaped nipple.

Ferrules are located at the ends of the outer cable, with the outer cable fitted inside of the ferrules.

The **outer cable** will be one continuous length for the front brake, typically in two separate lengths for rear rim brakes and three separate lengths for rear disc brakes (to reduce friction, weight and effects of cable compression) as follows:

- the first part is from the brake lever to the front of the top tube of the frame;
- the second from the rear of the top tube to either the rim brake caliper or to the top of the seat-stay;
- the third (for disc brakes only) from the bottom of the seat-stay to the disc brake caliper.

Grommets (or donuts) are optional rubber discs placed on runs of bare cable to stop the cable rattling against the frame.

An **end cap** is crimped to the end of cable to prevent it fraying.

When considering **cable length**, the inner cable needs to be a continuous cable that is long enough to reach from the brake lever to either the front or rear caliper (note: a longer inner cable will be required for a disc brake – check the measurement before you buy). You will also need sufficient outer cable for all the different pieces for both front and rear brakes. (Note that some bikes may require a single continuous piece of outer cable for the rear brake.)

Frame fitment options include:

- **Internal routing**, whereby the rear inner cable is routed through the inside of the frame top tube;
- **External routing with cable-stops**, whereby the outer cable terminates within cable-stops that are integral to the frame;
- **External routing with cable attachment points** - used where there is a continuous run of outer cable from the brake lever to the caliper that is attached to the frame at a number of points by clips or cable ties.

Brake cable specifications options include:

- Teflon-coated and/or polished inner cables;
- Outer cables with low-friction linings;
- Kevlar-reinforced outer cables;
- Specific cable-kits that have outer cables with end sections for routing under the bar-tape with drop handlebars.

Brake outer cables are available in a wide range of **colours**, which have a high level of visual impact for the bike – choose carefully!

You may also wish to coordinate the **brands** of components (e.g. using Campagnolo cables if you have a full Campagnolo groupset).

Note that brake inner cables have a thicker diameter (1.6mm) than gear cables (1-1.2mm) and are not interchangeable.

Note also, that brake outer cables have a different construction to gear outer cables are also a wider diameter (5mm vs. 4mm). They are not interchangeable; brake cables are subject to much higher compressive forces than gear cables.

Brake Hoses for Hydraulic Brakes are continuous pipes containing hydraulic fluid and transmit the force from the brake lever to the brake caliper. Typically, hoses are supplied ready-assembled to the brake lever and caliper. Should you need or wish to procure separately, you will need to consider the following:

- Brake hose assembly parts;
- Hose length;
- Frame fitment and routing;
- Hose specification, brand and colour.

Brake hose assemblies consist of a number of separate parts, as illustrated below.

The **barb (or insert)** is screwed or inserted (depending on make) into the end of the hose to provide rigidity and forms the sealing face for the pipe.

The **olive** slides onto the hose and is compressed by the nut to form a seal for the joint.

There is a **nut** at either end of the hose, it is supplied with the lever or caliper and is tightened to compress the olive to form the seal.

The **hose** is usually supplied at a length to suit the longest potential installation, so it is likely that it will be too long for your bike and therefore will need cutting to the correct size. After cutting, a new barb and olive will need to be used to minimise the risk of fluid leaks.

Some calipers use a **banjo** connection method with the associated **bolt** and **O-rings**.

Frame routing is either internal or external:

- **Internal routing** will require hoses to be disconnected such that they can be routed through the frame and/or forks, which could be done as a concurrent task to shortening the hose and bleeding the system.
- **External routing** requires bosses on the frame for attaching the hose securely.

Hose specifications can vary, specifically the internal diameter of the hose – ensure you match the hose to the specifications of the brake lever and caliper. Where possible, also match the make of hose to that of the lever and caliper.

Brake hoses are typically black, however other **colours** are available – but not as many as with brake cables.

Gear Cables and Wires

Cable-operated (mechanical) gears typically have a single cable for each of the front and rear gear systems that connects the gear shifter to the mechanism. You will need to consider the following parameters when selecting the cables:

- Gear cable assembly parts;
- Cable length;
- Cable adjustment;
- Frame fitment and routing;
- Cable specification, brand and colour.

Gear cable assemblies consist of a number of separate parts, as illustrated below.

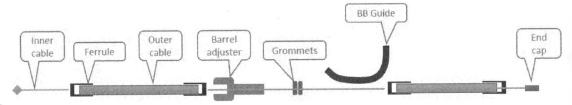

The **inner cable** connects to the gear shifter and has a nipple at the end of the cable – usually the same for road and MTB.

Ferrules are located at the ends of the outer cable.

The **outer cable** will typically be a single length for the front gear and typically in two lengths for the rear gear (some bikes have a continuous run of rear outer cable):

- the first part is from the gear shifter to the front of the down tube (road bike) or top tube (MTB) of the frame;
- the second from the end of the chain or seat-stay to the rear mech;

Some bike frames have threaded cable stops at the front of the top or down tube, which accept a **barrel adjuster** – this enables an easy method of adjustment for the gear cable.

Grommets (or donuts) are optional rubber discs placed on runs of bare cable to reduce rattles.

A **bottom bracket guide** is fitted to frames that route the gear cables along the down tube and under the bottom bracket – there are various shapes and sizes available, check the frame specification to see if you need to procure one and the relevant type.

An **end cap** is crimped to the end of cable to prevent it fraying.

When considering **cable length**, the inner cable needs to be a continuous cable that is long enough to reach from the gear shifter to either the front or rear mech. You will also need sufficient outer cable for all the different pieces for both front and rear brakes. (Note that some bikes may require a single continuous piece of outer cable for the rear gear.)

Cable Adjustment

Road bike shifters don't typically have any cable adjustment features, therefore if the bike doesn't accept a barrel adjuster (e.g. internal routed cables), then an inline adjuster will need to be fitted to make fine adjustments for the front mech. Note that some newer front mechs (e.g. Shimano R8000) offer cable tension adjustment). Flat bar gear shifters typically have a barrel adjuster as part of the lever assembly. Rear mechs also typically have a barrel adjuster built-in.

It can also be useful to fit an inline adjuster to the rear gear cable on a road bike such that you can make fine adjustments whilst riding.

Frame fitment options include:

- **Internal routing,** whereby both inner cables are routed through the inside of either the frame top tube or down tube.
- **External routing with cable-stops,** whereby the outer cable terminates within cable-stops that are integral to the frame. (Typically on a road bike, the front cable stop will be threaded for a barrel adjuster).
- **External routing with cable attachment points,** where there is a continuous run of outer cable from the gear shifter to the mech that is attached to the frame at a number of points by clips or cable ties.

Note that there are two standards for routing for front gear cables:

- **Bottom-pull,** where the front gear cable routes along the down tube and via the bottom bracket guide to the front mech - pulling downwards (most road bikes use this method);
- **Top-pull,** where the front gear cable routes along the top tube and down the initial part of the seat tube to the front mech - pulling upwards (most mountain bikes use this method).

Gear cable specifications options include:

- Teflon-coated and/or polished inner cables;
- Outer cables with low-friction linings;
- Kevlar-reinforced outer cables;
- Specific cable-kits that have outer cables with end sections for routing under the bar-tape with drop handlebars.

Gear outer cables are available in a wide range of **colours**, which have a high level of visual impact for the bike – choose carefully!

You may also wish to coordinate the **brands** of components (e.g. using Campagnolo cables if you have a full Campagnolo groupset).

For **electronic gear systems**, you will need to follow the instructions relevant to the make of system, this may also involve using the seatpost to house the battery and the use of multiple sections of wires to interconnect the various components.

Dropper Seatpost Cables and Hoses

Typically, a dropper seatpost will be supplied as a complete unit along with the remote lever and cable or hose. The parameters to check, or consider if you are making changes are:

- Cable/hose length;
- Cable/hose routing;
- Colour.

Length

For the initial fit, you will probably need to shorten the cable/hose to fit the bike; this is fairly straightforward for a cable, but will require a new barb/insert and olive for a hose (spares are usually supplied with the unit). For a replacement, you will need to measure the old cable/hose and cut to length accordingly.

Routing

Please refer to the Frame and Forks section - additional considerations for MTB for cable/hose routing and also the Saddle and Seatpost section for remote control mounting.

Note: if you need to internally-route a hydraulic hose it will need disconnecting and re-bleeding afterwards – you may also need to shorten the hose, which will also require a new barb/insert and olive.

Colour

Dropper seatposts are usually supplied with a black cable/hose, but you may wish to change this if you have a different target colour scheme.

Cables, Hoses and Wire Detailed Specification

Before proceeding, please write down your answers for the following questions:

1) Have you included all the components you will need for brake cables/hoses (and sufficient lengths of cable)?
2) Have you included all the components you will need for gear cables (and sufficient lengths of cable)?
3) Do you understand all the cable, hose or wire routing and frame attachment methods?
4) Do you need any specialist tools or spares (e.g. bleed kit)?
5) Do all of the colours (and logos) align with the intended scheme of the bike?

Pedals and Shoes

This chapter will guide you through choosing pedals and shoes to meet your needs. The first step is to determine the pedal type, as per the following flow chart.

The key decision is whether you wish your feet to be securely attached to the pedals, via various means, or whether you want flat pedals that allow you to take your foot away from the pedal without having to disengage your shoe from the pedal first. (Note: the term "clipless" is misleading – you still "clip-in" to the pedal, but using a mechanism under the shoe rather than an old-style toe-clip with a strap).

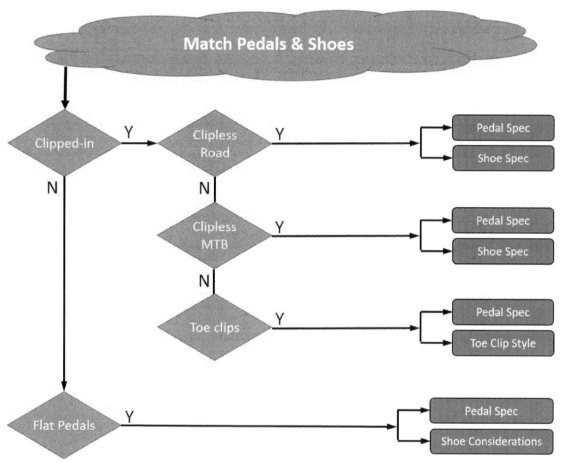

Regarding each pedal type:

1. **Clipless Road pedals** are generally lighter than MTB pedals and use a cleat that protrudes from the sole of the shoe to engage with the pedal, which makes walking awkward.
2. **Clipless MTB pedals** are more tolerant of muddy conditions and are usually easier to clip in and out. The cleats are usually recessed in the shoe, making walking easier. Note that many people also choose this type of pedal for road, gravel and hybrid bikes.
3. **Toe clips** (once the only method of securing your feet to the pedals but now largely replaced by clipless designs) attach to flat pedals and can be used with or without a strap to secure the foot.
4. **Flat pedals** have no mechanism for securing a shoe, although some types are available with long pins to provide a high level of traction with the sole of the shoe.

The table below summarise the pros and cons of each type of pedal.

Pedal Type	Advantages	Disadvantages
Clipless Road	Direct contact with bike, foot less likely to slip off pedal. Typically lighter than clipless MTB pedals. Longer cleat gives a stiffer interface. Precise location of foot on pedal.	Typically slower to disengage than clipless MTB system. Walking is awkward and will wear the cleat. Not very tolerant of dirt. Needs specific shoes.
Clipless MTB	Direct contact with bike, foot less likely to slip off pedal. Typically easier and quicker to disengage than clipless road system. Walking is easier, more tolerant of dirt. Precise location of foot on pedal.	You are still clipped-in, so not as fast/easy to put feet down as compared to flat pedals. Needs specific shoes (different from clipless road).
Toe Clips (with strap)	Direct contact with bike, foot less likely to slip on pedal. Good location of foot on pedal. No specific shoe requirement.	Hands are needed to tighten and loosen strap, so much slower to extract feet compare to clipless options. Limited choice available.
Toe Clips (strapless)	Helps with good foot location on pedal. Easier to put feet down than above. No specific shoe requirement.	Potential for feet to slip off pedals.
Flat Pedals	Easy to put feet down. No specific shoe requirement.	No location guide for foot position. Feet can slip off pedals when wet and bounce off pedals over rough terrain.

Ideally, see if you can test-ride the different systems or solicit opinions from others to make your choice.

Regarding shoes and cleats for clipless systems, the following diagram highlights the differences.

Road – uses a three-bolt mounting pattern, with the cleat protruding from the sole of the shoe.

MTB – uses a two-bolt mounting pattern, typically with the cleat recessed within the tread of the shoe.

Combination – some shoes are available with both bolt patterns so cleats from either system can be used, however the cleats will protrude from the sole whichever option is used.

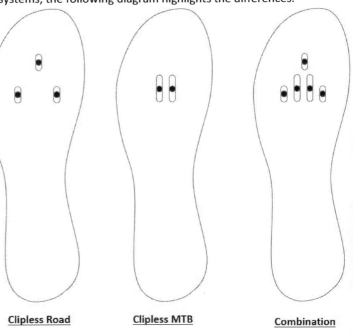

Clipless Road   Clipless MTB   Combination

The key parameters to consider for pedals and shoes are illustrated in the following flow chart; these will be discussed for each type of pedal.

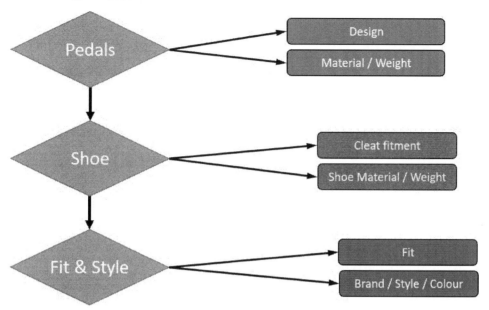

Clipless Road Pedals

There are various **designs** of clipless road pedals, with companies such as Shimano, Look, Time and Ritchey providing a one-sided design (the binding mechanism is just on one side of the pedal and the pedal is weighted to hang in a nose-up position to aid engaging the cleat); whilst Speedplay has a design with the binding attached to the shoe and a two-sided pedal with a cleat structure.

Various **materials** are used for pedals and cleats. Pedal axles are made from steel for lower-cost pedals and titanium for premium pedals. Pedal bodies range from plastic through to carbon fibre, which are sometimes fitted with steel plates to reduce wear.

Pedal **weight** typically ranges from 350g for entry-level pedals and cleats down to 130g for the lightest on the market.

Clipless Road Shoes

The main objective of road shoes is to provide a rigid platform for the foot on the pedal at as low a weight as feasible. As described previously, clipless road shoes use a three-bolt mounting system for cleats, which is common across the different makes of pedals (the cleat is different but can be replaced with a different type on the same shoe).

Shoe **materials** also vary - typically with price. Road shoes have a rigid sole with carbon fibre used on premium shoes. Shoe fastening features range from basic Velcro straps on entry-level shoes, with ratchet closures on mid-range shoes and dials with wire lacing on premium shoes.

Shoe **weight** is often overlooked, but worth paying attention to, especially if you are try to shed every gram from the bike itself. Road shoes can vary from over 700g down to around 400g per pair.

Clipless MTB Pedals

Clipless MTB pedals are designed to aid rapid cleat engagement, and either have rotational symmetry (i.e. the same design is presented on both sides of the pedal) or are different on each side of the pedal (e.g. one side with a binding and the other side a flat pedal platform).

There is also a wide range of designs available from wide platforms down to minimalistic clip mechanisms (such as the Crank Brothers Eggbeater, which offers 4-sided engagement).

As with road pedals, **materials** become more exotic with higher prices, using titanium for spindles and bodies.

Pedal **weight** typically ranges from over 550g per pair for wider platform pedals and cleats down to 200g per pair for the lightest on the market.

Clipless MTB Shoes

The main objective of MTB shoes, as well as to provide a rigid platform, is to provide protection for the feet against the terrain and elements encountered when riding mountain bikes. MTB Shoes use a two-bolt cleat mounting system, which is a common standard across the different makes of pedals.

MTB shoes tend to be much heavier-duty than road shoes, but there is a much greater variety of types of shoes available, including lighter weight carbon fibre cyclocross shoes, winter-specific shoes with thermal and waterproofing features and downhill-style shoes with additional toe and ankle protection.

The weight of MTB shoes varies considerably, depending on intended use and materials, from around 1.2kg down to under 700g per pair.

Toe Clips

As mentioned previously, toe clips are available in two styles, namely: toe clips with straps and strapless toe clips, as illustrated in the adjacent diagram.

Toe clips with straps are available as either complete units (with the toe clips as an integral part of the pedal), or bolt-on accessories that can be fitted to flat pedals (providing holes exist for the fixing bolts).

Strapless Toe Clips are fitted as bolt-on accessories to flat pedals (providing holes exist) and can be used as a transition from flat pedals to either toe clips with straps or clipless pedals.

Toe Clip with Strap

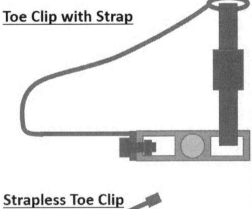

Strapless Toe Clip

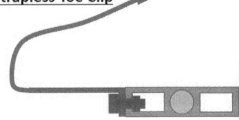

Flat Pedals

Flat pedals are available in a range of shapes and sizes, but with two main styles available, as illustrated below.

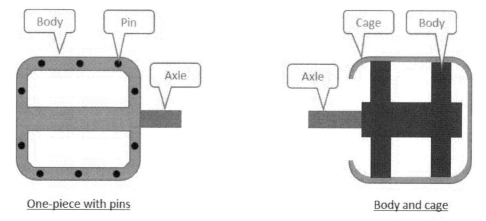

One-piece with pins   Body and cage

1) **One-piece pedals**, made from a single plastic moulding or metal casting with pins for grip;
2) **Body and Cage pedals** (also termed "Beartrap") which have an H-shaped central support surrounded by a U-shaped serrated cage.

One-piece pedals are the most common type, with budget pedals made from plastic with moulded pins (non-replaceable) and steel axles; through to titanium and magnesium bodies with adjustable and replaceable pins and with titanium axles.

If you wish to fit toe-clips, then typically you will need a body-and-cage design of pedal, but check for compatibility with toe-clips before you order.

Another feature to be aware of is the bearing specification for pedals:

- Budget pedals will typically have a single bearing and a bush;
- Premium pedals will have two or even three bearings, providing smoother rotation and longer life.

Pedal **weight** varies with material. Heavy-duty aluminium alloy pedals will typically weigh up to 600g, plastic-moulded pedals will weigh around 350g, and premium magnesium/titanium pedals will be less than 300g.

Shoes for Flat Pedals

As there is no specific engagement mechanism between the pedal and the shoe, you have freedom to choose whichever shoes you like! There are however shoes available specifically (e.g. Five Ten) for riding with flat pedals; the features of such shoes include:

- Flat and wide sole to maximise contact with the pedal (minimal tread on the shoe in the "pedal zone");
- Sole material with a soft yet durable texture, to provide traction with the pedal pins but resist damage from the pins;
- Additional protection for toes and ankles;
- Waterproofing.

Fit and Style

As pedals and shoes are another "extremity" item, they are available in a range of **colours** and have an impact on the bike and rider's visual appearance, so choose carefully to align with your colour scheme.

As with all shoes, **fit** will vary between makes and not necessarily align with any of your other shoes, so try before you buy (or be prepared to buy a selection of sizes and return those that don't fit). Also take into account the thickness of socks you intend to wear – especially for riding in cold weather.

Regarding your **riding position**, if you are going to be clipped-in then the position of the cleat on the sole of the sole can affect your riding efficiency, comfort and even cause injury if incorrect – there is a wealth of information on the internet to advise you further, or you may choose to have a bike-fit to help set up the cleats correctly.

A further consideration is the degree of **"float"** with clipless systems – this is the degree of free lateral rotation of the shoe within the mechanism, which can cause knee issues if excessive or insufficient for your natural pedal motion. Some manufacturers offer adjustment within the pedal mechanism, others provide a range of different cleats offering different amounts of float. This is a fairly complex subject with differing expert opinions and may not cause you any issues, or may be best addressed through a bike-fit.

Note that cleats are usually supplied with the pedals and are not typically interchangeable between different makes of pedal.

Pedals and Shoes Detailed Specification

Before proceeding, please write down your answers for the following questions:

1) What type of pedals will you use?
2) What are the specification details for the pedals (make, material, weight)?
3) Do the shoes match the cleat format of the pedals?
4) What are the specification details for the shoes (size, make, material, weight)?
5) Do all of the colours (and logos) align with the intended scheme of the bike?

Accessories

The accessories that you may wish to consider include:

- Drink bottle cage;
- Mudguards;
- Lights;
- Aero/tri bars;
- Spares and tools to carry whilst riding;
- GPS Device.

Drink Bottle Cage

For longer rides, it will be essential to take a drink with you to keep you hydrated. The choice for carrying the drink is either:

- Bike mounted, or
- Body mounted.

Bike mounted involves attaching one, two or more bottle cages to the frame (and/or saddle or handlebars) – attaching to the bosses integral to the frame structure as relevant. Cage materials range from alloy and plastic through to carbon fibre and titanium. Although the capacity of drinks bottles vary, the majority of drinks bottles are the same diameter and have recesses at the same distance from the base enabling inter-compatibility between bottles and cages.

Body mounted would either involve carrying water bottles in jersey pockets or the use of a hydration back-pack.

Mudguards

There is a wide range of mudguards available; the table below compares and contrasts common formats.

Format	Pros	Cons	Typical Usage
Full-length bolt-on	Good level of protection for rider, bike and fellow cyclists (if long enough)	Time consuming to fit and remove. Can be expensive & heavy. Require mounting points on frame/forks.	Commuting, Winter bike, Winter group riding.
Full-length clip-on	Good protection Don't need frame/fork mounting points	Less sturdy/durable than bolt-on	Summer bike Winter group riding
Partial-length	Easy to fit/remove Some level of protection	Limited protection No protection for other cyclists	Any bike, front and rear
Stubby (e.g. Ass-saver)	Easy to fit/remove Will fit in pocket Better than no mudguard	Very limited protection	Any bike (attaches under the saddle)

Lights

The key decision with lights is whether you need lights that are:

- Bright enough to be seen safely, or
- Bright enough to illuminate the path/road ahead (typically over 400 lumens)

If you typically ride on roads and only occasionally after dark, then the former category is probably ok. It is also advisable to use lights on a bike during the daytime if the light-levels are reduced.

If you plan to ride for significant periods after dark, or plan to ride off-road, then you will need the second category – also consider multiple lights in case of light/battery failure during a ride.

Key features of bike lights include:

- Rechargeable lights – typically with USB charging connectors;
- Battery life indication;
- Variable output – e.g. brightest setting when you need it, reduced output to save power otherwise;
- Variable mode – e.g. constant brightness and different flashing patterns;
- Helmet mounting (usually in addition to bike-mounted lights);
- Mounting type – clamps for a more secure fitting, elastic straps for easy changes;
- Remote battery - keeping the light itself compact and low in weight with a cable that connects to the battery pack - either both mounted on the bike or with the light on your helmet and the battery in a pocket.

Aero/Tri Bars

If you have a regular road bike and wish to use the bike in a time-trial or triathlon event, you may wish to fit bolt-on aero/tri bars to your existing handlebars.

Various profiles are available – if possible try-before-you-buy.

Some models are adjustable, others are fixed in length.

Generally, aero-tri bars are made from aluminium alloy, but carbon fibre bars are available if you prefer.

Note that your gear & brake controls will remain on the existing handlebars, so you will have to change hand position accordingly to brake or shift.

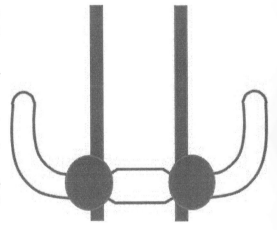

Spares and Tools to Carry

The essentials to take with you on a ride are:

- One inner tube (two on longer rides or in adverse conditions) – or a tubeless tyre repair kit;
- Tyre levers;
- Pump or CO2 inflators (can either be bike-mounted or carried in a jersey pocket);
- Allen keys (3mm, 4mm, 5mm and 6mm) or a multi-tool.

Further recommended items, especially for longer rides, are:

- Puncture repair patches (self-adhesive are easier to use on a ride);
- Spoke key (if you know how to use one to straighten a wheel);
- Chain tool with spare quick-links and/or pins.

GPS Device

There is a wide range of GPS devices available with a spectrum of features to choose from, such as:

- Ride data recording (which can then be uploaded to your chosen tracking software);
- Route navigation (ranging from turn-by-turn following a "breadcrumb trail" through to detailed mapping, similar to an automotive Sat-Nav);
- Bluetooth connectivity (uploads through your phone and shows alerts for calls and messages);
- Long battery life (important if you plan to do long-distance rides);
- Heart rate monitoring;
- Cadence and wheel speed monitoring;
- Power monitoring (if you have a power meter);
- Colour screen;
- Touch screen;
- Integration with electronic groupsets
- Various mounting options.

Determine your "must-have" list of features and choose accordingly.

The Complete Low Level Specification

You have covered all the component groups of a bike, so now need to:

1) Calculate the total cost;
2) Calculate the total weight;
3) Read relevant magazine or consumer reviews to inform your final product decisions;
4) Revisit components accordingly to refine the cost and/or weight if necessary – benchmarking against the worked examples as relevant;
5) Confirm your colour-scheme (see below regarding virtual visualisation) and logo-matching;
6) Write a shopping list for all the items you need to buy, using the table on the following page;;
7) Add any accessories to the list as relevant.

Virtual Visualisation

To help you select your desired colour scheme for the bike, there are a number of websites that allow you to model the bike and visualise the result, such as:

http://www.bikeconfig.com/

http://varsitybike.com/bikes/color-your-bike/

http://www.pedalmafia.com/mafid/mafia_id.html

https://www.bikecad.ca/

Final Component Choices

From the specification decisions made during the Low Level Design, you will either have selected definitive components (e.g. a particular frame or a groupset) or you may still be at a more generic specification level (e.g. carbon fibre seatpost, which is 27.2mm diameter, 350mm long and with 20mm set-back). For the latter, you should make your final product selection as part of the procurement process when considering price and supplier/delivery factors.

Write a shopping list

Grouping	Component	Cost	Weight (g)	Specification
Frameset	Frame			
	Rear Shock			
	Shock mountings			
	Forks			
	Compression Device			
	Headset			
Groupset	Shifters			
	Front Mech			
	Rear Mech			
	Chainset			
	Bottom bracket			
	Cassette			
	Chain			
	Front brake caliper			
	Rear brake caliper			
	Caliper mounting			
	Brake rotors			
Wheels & Tyres	Front Wheel			
	Front QR / Axle			
	Rear Wheel			
	Rear QR / Axle			
	Tyres			
	Tubes			
	Valves & Rim tape			
	Tyre sealant			
Ancillaries	Bars			
	Bar tape / Grips			
	Stem			
	Headset spacers			
	Saddle			
	Seatpost			
	Seatpost clamp			
	Gear outer cable			
	Brake cables / hoses			
	Chain guide			
	Pedals			
	Total			

5. Procurement

Selecting Deals

With your shopping list now ready for both the bike and accessories you are now ready to search out the best deals. This will typically involve a lot of internet searching; the main considerations will include:

- **Special offers** – if possible monitor the prices of the high-value items over a period of time (or consult with others) to be able to spot a good offer.

- **Discount codes** – you may have access to discount codes from either previous purchases, promotional emails or memberships (e.g. British Cycling offers a 10% discount code for Halfords, Evans and Chain Reaction Cycles).

- **Ex-display items** – as an example you may find a heavily-discounted set of forks that has been cut-to-length for a bike and then swapped without being used.

- **Price Match** - many retailers will price-match with others - but check the small-print.

- **Cycle-to-Work Schemes** can be very cost effective (saving tax + N.I. and spreading the payments over a year) if the circumstances align for you; but typically the discount is off the Recommended Retail Price (RRP) rather than a sale-price and many companies have a maximum limit of £1000 for a complete bike only (although this limit has now been removed). The scheme usually only runs for a limited time period each year and there is a variety of schemes, each applicable to different retailers.

- Check **cycling magazines** and **internet search engines** for deals on specific components.

- Check and plan for **delivery** costs and timescales. The best deal might be directly from China but involve several weeks' delivery.

Warranty

Before you buy, take the time to read the small-print regarding any warranties offered on either complete bikes or components. Many warranty policies cover against manufacturing faults (e.g. a crack in a weld soon after purchase) but exclude anything relating to "wear and tear", which could be interpreted as a crack in a weld after a longer time period of use.

It may also be worth reading user-posts on cycling forums to check for real-life experience of warranty claims.

Some companies honour a life-time warranty on their frames, others are limited to a finite period.

Worked Examples

Before you start the ordering process, review the most relevant of the following worked examples to benchmark your component choices, costs and weights.

1) Low-spec road bike;
2) Mid-spec road bike;
3) High-spec road bike;
4) Gravel bike;
5) Low-spec Hardtail MTB;
6) Mid-spec Hardtail MTB;
7) Low-spec Full Suspension MTB.
8) Mid-spec Full Suspension MTB.

These worked examples should also help you with the decision of whether to buy a complete bike or to source the parts separately and build the bike yourself; bearing in mind that a complete bike will tend to be cheaper than the sum of the parts but may not give you the exact specification you want.

Another key factor in the build/buy decision will be whether you already have a number of components from other bikes that you plan to reuse.

The worked examples also correspond to the high level target cost and weights earlier in the book and now include a full breakdown of the corresponding specifications. A summary of the examples is included below with key observations listed.

Example	Cost	Weight	Notes
Low-spec road	£745	9.54kg	If you choose the deals carefully, then this is a viable approach for a self-build.
Mid-spec road	£1,650	7.93kg	Probably cheaper to buy a complete bike - but only if you are happy with the stock specification.
High-spec road	£4,540	6.46kg	At this price-point, you will need to be clear whether you want a complete bike from a specific brand, or whether you really want to tailor the specification such that you will need to source the components separately and build yourself (or get someone else to build it for you).
Gravel bike	£2,006	9.39kg	This is the most complicated example specification, so it all depends if you can find a good deal on a suitable frameset (e.g. carbon fibre). If not, then buy a complete bike and change the relevant components as you require.
Low-spec Hardtail	£1,027	12.6kg	If you choose the deals carefully, then this is a viable approach for a self-build.
Mid-spec Hardtail	£2,487	11.4kg	There isn't much choice for carbon hardtail frames, so you will probably get a better deal buying a complete bike - but a self-build may be viable if you already own a number of key components.
Low-spec Full-Sus	£1,802	14.5kg	Probably cheaper to buy a complete bike unless you can't find the specification you want or if you spot a stunning deal. Also worth considering if you already have a lot of parts to re-use.
Mid-spec Full-Sus	£3,337	13.2kg	

Worked Example: Low-Spec Road Bike (Target £750, 9.5kg)

The objective for this specification is to achieve a good functioning bike without cutting any corners nor with excess weight by choosing good value, mainstream components and component combinations, such as complete groupsets. The component costs, weights and specification rationale are detailed in the table below.

Grouping	Component	Cost	Weight (g)	Specification Rationale
Frameset	Frame	£150	1,700	6061 or 7005 Aluminium alloy frame, Carbon-bladed fork, alloy steerer – bought as a frameset (e.g. from Chain Reaction, Planet X or Ribble)
	Forks		650	
	Headset	£15	100	Some framesets will include the headset
Groupset	Shifters	£300	2,600	Either Shimano Tiagra or SRAM Apex Complete Groupset
	Front Mech			
	Rear Mech			
	Chainset			
	Bottom bracket			
	Cassette			
	Chain			
	Front brake caliper			
	Rear brake caliper			
Wheels & Tyres	Front Wheel	£120	2,000	Good brand, low-spec wheelset (e.g. Fulcrum Racing Sport)
	Front QR			
	Rear Wheel			
	Rear QR			
	Tyres	£25	600	There is usually plenty of choice of discounted big-brand tyres
	Tubes	£10	160	
Ancillaries	Bars	£20	350	6061 alloy
	Bar tape	£10	80	
	Stem	£15	160	6061 alloy
	Headset spacers	£3	20	
	Saddle	£15	300	
	Seatpost	£15	300	6061 alloy
	Seatpost clamp	£5	30	
	Gear outer cable	£5	40	Gear inner cables usually supplied with shifters
	Brake cables	£12	100	Probably need to buy both inner and outer brake cables
	Pedals	£25	350	e.g. Shimano R540 SPD-SL
	Total	**£745**	**9,540**	

Worked Example: Mid-Spec Road Bike (Target £1700, 8kg)

The objective for this specification is to achieve a lightweight bike with a good specification whilst also choosing good value, mainstream components and component combinations, such as complete wheelsets and groupsets. The component costs, weights and specification rationale are detailed in the table below.

Grouping	Component	Cost	Weight (g)	Specification Rationale
Frameset	Frame	£500	1,100	Full carbon frame and forks from high-volume retailer (e.g. Planet X or Ribble)
	Forks		350	
	Compression Device	£10	50	
	Headset	£50	80	
Groupset	Shifters	£530	2,400	E.g. Shimano Ultegra R8000 (mechanical/rim brakes - Hydraulic disc brakes will cost and weigh more)
	Front Mech			
	Rear Mech			
	Chainset			
	Bottom bracket			
	Cassette			
	Chain			
	Front brake caliper			
	Rear brake caliper			
Wheels & Tyres	Front Wheel	£400	1,700	Lightweight alloy wheelset bundle with tyres (e.g. Fulcrum Racing 3)
	Front QR			
	Rear Wheel			
	Rear QR			
	Tyres		450	
	Tubes		160	
Ancillaries	Bars	£20	350	6061 alloy
	Bar tape	£10	70	
	Stem	£15	160	6061 alloy
	Headset spacers	£3	20	
	Saddle	£15	300	
	Seatpost	£50	220	Carbon fibre seatpost
	Seatpost clamp	£5	30	
	Gear outer cable	£5	40	Gear inner cables usually supplied with shifters
	Brake cables	£12	100	Probably need to buy both inner and outer brake cables
	Pedals	£25	350	e.g. Shimano R540 SPD-SL
	Total	**£1,650**	**7,930**	

Note: the above specification uses the same handlebars, stem, saddle and pedals as the Low-Spec Road Bike in order to keep the price down. If you wish, these could be upgraded as follows:

Component	Extra Cost	Weight Saving	Specification
Handlebars	£30	70g	7075 Aluminium Alloy
Stem	£25	30g	2014 Aluminium Alloy
Saddle	£35	50g	Wide choice of higher-spec saddles available
Pedals	£40	65g	e.g. Shimano 105 5800
Difference	**£130**	**215g**	
Total Bike	**£1,780**	**7,715g**	

Worked Example: High-Spec Road Bike (Target £4500, 6.7kg)

The objective for this specification is to achieve a very lightweight bike with a high level of specification whilst still using good-value component combinations, such as complete wheelsets and groupsets. The component costs, weights and specification rationale are detailed in the table below.

Grouping	Component	Cost	Weight (g)	Specification Rationale
Frameset	Frame	£1,500	1100	Lightweight branded carbon frame and forks
	Forks			
	Compression Device	£10	50	May be included with frameset
	Headset	£50	80	
Groupset	Shifters	£1,250	2000	E.g. Shimano Dura Ace 9100, Campagnolo Record or SRAM Red - or you could consider Shimano Ultegra (or equivalent) with hydraulic brakes and electronic shift – but will add weight
	Front Mech			
	Rear Mech			
	Chainset			
	Bottom bracket			
	Cassette			
	Chain			
	Front brake caliper			
	Rear brake caliper			
Wheels & Tyres	Front Wheel	£1,300	1450	Carbon wheelset bundle with tyres (e.g. Fulcrum Racing Zero)
	Front QR			
	Rear Wheel			
	Rear QR			
	Tyres		400	
	Tubes		110	
Ancillaries	Bars	£50	280	7075 alloy
	Bar tape	£20	55	e.g. Lizardskins DSP 2.5
	Stem	£40	130	2014 alloy
	Headset spacers	£10	15	Carbon fibre
	Saddle	£120	180	Carbon fibre saddle / rails
	Seat post	£50	220	Carbon fibre seatpost
	Seatpost clamp	£10	20	
	Gear outer cable	£30	120	e.g. Shimano Ultegra cable set
	Brake cables			
	Pedals	£100	250	e.g. Shimano Ultegra R8000
	Total	**£4,540**	**6460**	

Note that a significant proportion of the above specification is constructed from carbon fibre, the main exceptions being the handlebars and stem. Upgrading these to carbon fibre would add approximately £200 and save around 100g (not great value-for-money for weight-saving but may provide benefits for reducing vibrations and increasing the stiffness of the handlebars).

Worked Example: Gravel Bike (Target £2000, 9.5kg)

The objective for this specification is to achieve a multi-purpose bike with a good specification that can be ridden off-road (paths & non-technical trails) whilst maintaining the pace and long distance capability of a road bike – and also a great winter bike. The key features for the bike include:

- Hydraulic disc brakes;
- Tubeless tyres, with width 30-35mm and room for mudguards;
- Wide-ratio 1x11 Drivetrain for simplicity and coping with dirt;
- Thru axles (for rigidity and to eliminate risk of wheel-slip under heavy braking).

Grouping	Component	Cost	Weight (g)	Specification Rationale
Frameset	Frame	£600	1,700	6061 or 7005 Aluminium alloy frame (possibly carbon if special offer available)
	Forks		500	Full carbon fork
	Thru Axles		160	May be included with frameset (worth checking)
	Compression Device	£10	50	
	Headset	£50	80	
Groupset	Hydr. Shifters & Calipers	£400	800	E.g. SRAM Force
	Rear Mech	£85	270	E.g. SRAM Rival 1 Type 2.1 (11-speed)
	Chainset	£110	700	E.g. SRAM Rival 1 (42T)
	Bottom bracket	£20	110	E.g. SRAM GXP
	Cassette	£55	440	11-42 (11 speed)
	Chain	£25	250	11-speed
Wheels & Tyres	Front & Rear Wheels	£350	1,800	Alloy wheelset, disc brake, thru-axle, tubeless ready (622x19c - 29" MTB)
	Brake Rotors	£40	260	160mm Front, 140mm Rear
	Tyres	£90	650	E.g. Schwalbe G-One Speed 622x30
	Valves & Rim tape	£0	0	Usually included with wheels – but check
	Tyre Sealant	£15	100	
Ancillaries	Bars	£20	350	6061 alloy
	Bar tape	£10	80	
	Stem	£15	160	6061 alloy
	Headset spacers	£3	20	
	Saddle	£15	300	
	Seatpost	£50	210	Carbon fibre seatpost - more compliance
	Seatpost clamp	£5	30	
	Gear Outer cable	£3	20	Rear only, inner cable supplied with shifter
	Pedals	£35	350	e.g. Shimano M540 SPD
	Total	£2,006	9,390	

Note: further potential weight reductions could be achieved with the following changes:

Component	Extra Cost	Weight Saving	Specification
Carbon Frame	£0-£400	500g	Watch-out for special offers for carbon framesets
Carbon Crankset	£50	90g	e.g. SRAM Force CX1
Handlebars	£30	70g	7075 Aluminium Alloy
Stem	£25	30g	2014 Aluminium Alloy
Saddle	£35	50g	Wide choice of higher-spec saddles available
Difference	£140+	740g	
Total Bike	£2,146+	8,650g	

Worked Example: Low-Spec Hardtail (Target £1000, 13kg)

This will be a good functioning bike without cutting any corners nor with excess weight by choosing good value, mainstream components and component combinations, such as complete groupsets. The key features for the bike include:

- 27.5" wheels with clincher tyres, inner tubes & QR-axles (to reduce cost);
- 1x11 Drivetrain (e.g. 32-tooth chainring with 11-42 cassette);
- Hydraulic disc brakes with 160mm rotors;
- Entry-level air-sprung forks (low cost but minimising weight impact).

Grouping	Component	Cost	Weight (g)	Specification Rationale
Frameset	Frame	£180	2,000	6061 or 7005 Aluminium alloy frame
	Forks	£200	2,200	100mm air-spring fork
	Headset	£15	100	
Groupset	Gear Shifter	£340	120	E.g. Shimano SLX M7000 1x11
	Brake Levers & Calipers		600	
	Rear Mech		330	
	Chainset		720	
	Bottom bracket		80	
	Cassette		480	
	Chain		260	
	Brake Rotors		300	
Wheels & Tyres	Front & Rear Wheels	£140	2,100	Good brand, low-spec wheelset (e.g. Shimano MT35)
	Axle / QR Skewers			
	Tyres	£25	1,300	Usually plenty of choice of discounted big-brand tyres
	Tubes	£10	350	
Ancillaries	Bars	£15	350	6061 alloy
	Grips	£10	80	
	Stem	£15	160	6061 alloy
	Headset spacers	£2	10	
	Saddle	£15	300	
	Seatpost	£15	300	6061 alloy
	Seatpost clamp	£5	40	
	Gear outer cable	£5	60	Gear inner cable usually supplied with shifter
	Pedals	£35	350	e.g. Shimano M540 SPD
	Total	**£1,027**	**12,590**	

Worked Example: Mid-Spec Hardtail (Target £2,500, 11.5kg)

This is a much richer specification than the Low-Spec Hardtail and includes the following additional features.

- Tubeless wheels and tyres with Thru-axles;
- Dropper seatpost;
- Carbon fibre frame;
- Higher specification fork with longer travel;
- Higher specification groupset.

Grouping	Component	Cost	Weight (g)	Specification Rationale
Frameset	Frame	£700	1,600	Carbon Fibre frame
	Forks	£450	1,900	140mm air-sprung fork with range of damping controls
	Thru axles	£0	160	Usually included with the frame / fork
	Headset	£50	100	
Groupset	Gear Shifter	£470	120	e.g. Shimano XT M8000 1x11
	Brake Levers & Calipers		550	
	Rear Mech		275	
	Chainset		675	
	Bottom bracket		80	
	Cassette		480	
	Chain		260	
	Brake Rotors		300	
Wheels & Tyres	Front & Rear Wheels	£400	1,800	Tubeless compatible 27.5" with thru-axles
	Tyres	£60	1,200	Usually plenty of choice of discounted big-brand tyres
	Valves & Rim tape	£0	0	Usually included with wheels – but check
	Tyre Sealant	£10	100	
Ancillaries	Bars	£30	300	7075 alloy
	Grips	£20	40	
	Stem	£30	130	7075 alloy
	Headset spacers	£2	10	
	Saddle	£15	300	
	Seatpost	£180	550	Dropper Seatpost
	Seatpost clamp	£5	30	
	Gear outer cable	£5	60	Gear inner cable usually supplied with shifter
	Pedals	£60	340	e.g. Shimano XT M8000
	Total	**£2,487**	**11,360**	

Worked Example: Low-Spec Full-suspension (Target £1,800, 14.5kg)

This specification delivers a good functioning bike without cutting corners. Key specification decisions include:

- 27.5" wheels with clincher tyres & inner tubes (to reduce cost);
- Thru-axles to improve wheel retention and stiffness;
- 1x11 Drivetrain (e.g. 32-tooth chainring with 11-42 cassette);
- Entry-level dropper seatpost.

Grouping	Component	Cost	Weight (g)	Specification Rationale
Frameset	Frame + rear shock	£750	3700	Entry-level 6061 alloy frame with 140-160mm travel, including rear shock
	Forks	£330	2000	140-160mm air-spring fork
	Thru axles	£0	140	usually included with the frame / fork
	Headset	£15	100	
Groupset	Gear Shifter	£340	120	E.g. Shimano SLX M7000 1x11
	Brake Levers & Calipers		600	
	Rear Mech		330	
	Chainset		720	
	Bottom bracket		80	
	Cassette		480	
	Chain		260	
	Brake Rotors		300	
Wheels & Tyres	Front & Rear Wheels	£140	2100	Good brand, low-spec wheelset (e.g. Shimano MT35)
	Tyres	£25	1300	Usually plenty of choice of discounted big-brand tyres
	Tubes	£10	350	
Ancillaries	Bars	£15	350	6061 alloy
	Grips	£10	80	
	Stem	£15	150	6061 alloy
	Headset spacers	£2	10	
	Saddle	£15	300	
	Seat post	£90	600	Budget Dropper Seatpost
	Seatpost clamp	£5	30	
	Gear outer cable	£5	30	Gear inner cable usually supplied with shifters
	Pedals	£35	350	e.g. Shimano M540 SPD
	Total	**£1,802**	**14480**	

Worked Example: Mid-Spec Full-Suspension (Target £3,350, 13.3kg)

This improves on the specification of the Low-Spec Full-suspension bike and includes the following additional features:

- Tubeless wheels and tyres with Thru-axles;
- Higher specification frame, fork and shock;
- Higher specification groupset;
- Higher specification dropper seatpost.

Grouping	Component	Cost	Weight (g)	Specification Rationale
Frameset	Frame + rear shock	£1,500	3200	6061 alloy frame with 140-160mm travel, including rear shock
	Forks	£500	1900	140-160mm air-spring fork with range of damping controls
	Thru axles	£0	120	usually included with the frame / fork
	Headset	£50	100	
Groupset	Gear Shifter	£470	120	e.g. Shimano XT M8000 1x11
	Brake Levers & Calipers		550	
	Rear Mech		275	
	Chainset		675	
	Bottom bracket		80	
	Cassette		480	
	Chain		260	
	Brake Rotors		300	
Wheels & Tyres	Front & Rear Wheels	£400	1900	Tubeless compatible 27.5" with thru-axles
	Tyres	£60	1400	Usually plenty of choice of discounted big-brand tyres
	Valves & Rim tape	£0	0	Usually included with wheels - but check
	Tyre Sealant	£10	100	
Ancillaries	Bars	£30	300	7075 alloy
	Grips	£20	40	
	Stem	£30	130	7075 alloy
	Headset spacers	£2	10	
	Saddle	£15	300	
	Seat post	£180	550	Dropper Seatpost
	Seatpost clamp	£5	30	
	Gear outer cable	£5	30	Gear inner cable usually supplied with shifters
	Pedals	£60	340	e.g. Shimano XT M8000
	Total	**£3,337**	**13190**	

Putting it all together

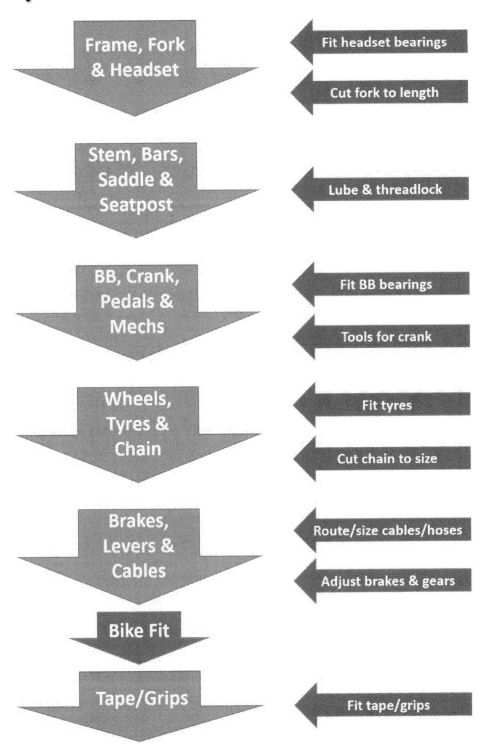

Frame, Fork & Headset

Fit headset bearings

Cut fork to length

Stem, Bars, Saddle & Seatpost

Lube & threadlock

BB, Crank, Pedals & Mechs

Fit BB bearings

Tools for crank

Wheels, Tyres & Chain

Fit tyres

Cut chain to size

Brakes, Levers & Cables

Route/size cables/hoses

Adjust brakes & gears

Bike Fit

Tape/Grips

Fit tape/grips

6. Building and Tuning Considerations

This book does not include step-by-step instructions for assembling a bike – this would be the subject of many separate books to cover the entire range of bike genres and standards. To help you understand the relative complexity, a basic sequence of assembly is illustrated in the diagram opposite.

The purpose of this chapter is to highlight the key tasks involved in building a bike (which may influence your "buy-whole or build" decision) and to inform you of the requirements for specialist tools. After reading this section, you may need to update your shopping list to include such tools and/or revise some of your component choices accordingly. The key topics described include:

- Fitting bearing cups and races;
- Cutting forks;
- Lubrication and threads;
- Fitting tyres (especially tubeless tyres);
- Chains;
- Brakes, hydraulic hoses and cables;
- Tuning the Bike to Fit.

If you do decide to build the bike, then consider buying a workstand to aid the process. Although very useful, you can still successfully build a bike without a workstand but it will involve turning the bike upside-down to stand on the handlebars and saddle in order to fit the BB, crank, gears and wheels.

Fitting Bearing Cups and Races

Headsets and bottom brackets are available in many formats (as described in the Low Level Design chapter) and require different methods and tools for assembly and removal.

(Note: the surest approach is to use the correct tool for each installation task, however various low-cost hack methods may also work effectively – do your research and proceed with caution.)

External and Internal (Semi-integrated) headsets have separate bearing cups which need to be pressed into the frame. Specific tools are available for this task that ensure a proper installation without risking damage to the frame or bearing cups.

Integrated headsets do not have separate bearing cups; the bearings are a loose-fit and do not require any tools for installation or removal.

Threaded bottom brackets require specific tools for tightening or undoing the bearing cups and cartridges. These tools are relatively inexpensive.

Press-fit bottom brackets, as the name implies, require the use of a specific press-tool (the same tool typically as used for headsets).

The **headset crown race** (mounts between the fork crown and the lower headset bearing) is either slotted, in which case can be fitted by hand, or is an interference-fit on the bottom of the steerer tube and therefore requires the use of a crown race setting tool.

Cutting Forks

Forks are typically made with a steerer tube at least long enough for the biggest frame size, so invariably the end of the steerer will need cutting down to the correct size for your needs – see adjacent diagram. Remember the old adage "measure twice, cut once" – if you cut the steerer tube too short then you will need to buy new forks!

The correct length is where there is a small amount (e.g. 2mm) of clearance between the top of the steerer tube and the underside of the top cap when the whole assembly is clamped together (including stem and desired spacers).

Alloy and carbon fibre forks can be cut easily with a hacksaw (steel can also be cut but check your saw-blade specification). Guide tools are available to help you cut clean and square, or you can use a spare headset spacer as a guide.

Use a safety mask when cutting carbon fibre to prevent inhalation of the loose fibres.

Clearance

Lubrication and Threads

The key rules for **tightening bolts** are:

1) If appropriate, use a thread-locking solution;
2) Use a correctly-fitting tool aligned correctly with the bolt;
3) Tighten to the correct torque.

Many bolts have a pre-applied **thread-lock** (especially stem and brake bolts), if re-using then re-apply as relevant. It is generally safe and good practice to apply a medium-strength thread-lock (nothing stronger) to most bolts on a bike, but avoid the following:

- Titanium or aluminium bolts;
- Wheel and crank axles – use grease instead;
- Pedals – use grease instead;
- Crank bolts – use grease instead;
- Seatpost clamp – use grease instead.

Where possible use a good-quality socket-insert **tool** (as per adjacent illustration) for tightening bolts rather than "L-shaped" Alley keys (although some bolts will only be accessible with an Allen key). The typical sizes of bolt you will find on a bike are:

Internal hex-head (Allen bolts):

- 2mm, 2.5mm, 3mm, 4mm, 5mm, 6mm, 8mm (pedals and cranks), 10mm (some cranks)

Internal Torx bolts:

- T10 (e.g. SRAM bleed port screw), T25

External hex-head:

- 8mm, 9mm, 10mm, 13mm, 15mm, 17mm

Screw head:

- Small and medium Phillips (e.g. derailleur limit screws)
- Small flat-blade (e.g. derailleur limit screws)

To obtain the correct **tightening torque**, use a good-quality torque wrench.

As well as using the correct tools for assembly, also take note of the **thread direction** (see diagram).

For English/BSA bottom brackets, the left bearing has right-hand thread and the right bearing has a left-hand thread.

For Italian bottom brackets, both sides have a right-hand thread.

For pedals, the right pedal has a right-hand thread, the left pedal has a left-hand thread.

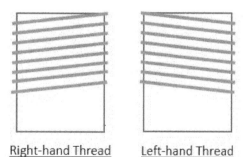

Right-hand Thread   Left-hand Thread

Note for Lubricating Seatposts and Stems

A common issue with seatposts is that they can seize in the frame tube, meaning that the saddle height cannot be adjusted and the seatpost cannot be removed. Stems can also seize onto the fork steerer tube. Seizing will occur between different materials (especially an aluminium alloy post in a steel frame, but also either combination of aluminium alloy and carbon). The best method of prevention is to use a barrier substance to prevent corrosion occurring. For non-carbon installations, a layer of grease will provide a suitable barrier. If one or both materials are carbon fibre then apply carbon assembly paste, which will reduce the risk of seizing and also improve the clamping of the joint, reducing the likelihood of slippage.

Fitting Tyres

Conventional clincher tyres should not present any issues regarding installation, however you may encounter issues if you intend to use tubeless tyres, such as:

1) Fitting the tyre to the rim;
2) Inflating the tyre;
3) Ensuring no leaks after initial inflation.

The ease of **fitting the tyre** will depend on the relative sizes of the rim and the tyre. As the standards are fairly loose, you may have to rely on consumer reviews or trial and error. Soapy water can be applied to the tyre bead to help with the process and as the tyres are intended to be a tighter fit than clincher tyres, you may need to use (good quality) tyre levers, but at least there isn't the risk of pinching an inner tube.

To successfully **inflate the tyre**, the rate of air entering through the valve needs to be greater than the rate of air escaping between the rim and the tyre until the tyre seats completely on the rim (pushed into place by the increasing internal pressure). Sometimes the tyre will inflate on the first attempt; if you are not able to inflate the tyre due to air leakage, then the following measures may help:

- Remove the core from the valve to maximise air-entry;
- Use a pump intended for tubeless tyres, which has an air-storage chamber (or a garage-style car tyre inflator – but you will need a Schraeder-Presta valve adaptor);
- Add rim tape to increase the diameter of the wheel's rim bead;
- Fit an inner tube to seat the tyre on both sides, then carefully remove the inner tube whilst keeping one side of the tyre seated on the rim, then refit and try again.

After inflating the tyre, you may suffer from **air leaks**. To minimise the risk of this happening ensure:

- You have used a quality tubeless rim tape and that it has adhered correctly (if needed);
- The valve is tight and forms a good seal with the rim (and the rim tape if needed);
- Add the recommended quantity of tyre sealant and disperse thoroughly (spin and shake the wheel) after inflating. If there are minor air leaks after inflating, the tyre sealant should work to seal such leaks (you may see small amounts escaping during this process).

Fitting Chains

To reduce the length of the chain, you will need a chain tool. Universal tools will work with the majority of chains, however Campagnolo chains require a specific tool. The method of joining a new chain will depend on the make; most Shimano chains use a pin that requires a chain tool to insert, whilst SRAM and KMC use a master link that can be closed by hand.

When shortening a chain that is joined with a pin, always shorten the narrower end as the pin will be retained within the unused wider end plates. Note also the drive direction with the wider end leading the narrow end, as illustrated below. Also ensure the logos on the chain face away from the bike.

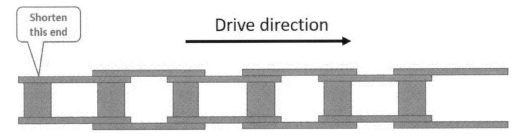

When shortening a chain that uses a master link, ensure both ends are narrow, as shown in the diagram below. Depending on the make of chain, some master links are directional and will have an arrow stamped on the sides of the link.

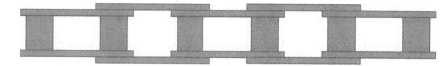

Regarding chain lubrication, new chains are pre-lubricated and this lubrication should be left on the chain with no need for further lubrication until necessary through usage.

Brakes, Hydraulic Hoses and Cables

If you plan to use **hydraulic** components, it is likely that you will have to shorten and/or internally-route brake or dropper seatpost hoses. If you cut a hose to shorten it, you will need to fit new seals (inserts/barbs and olives) – spares are usually included with new components, but not always. If you disconnect a hose (either for shortening or routing), it is likely that you will need to bleed the air out of the system afterwards.

Bleed kits will be required (some are provided with the components – e.g. RockShox seatposts), but you will need to match the bleed kit to the make of components. Also take care to buy the correct fluid for the system – refer back to the Low Level Design chapter.

Hose cutting tools are available that ensure a clean and square cut, however a craft knife can also be used if done carefully.

Brake and gear cable inners and outers will need cutting to length as part of a bike-build. Specific cable-cutting tools are available and advisable to use for this purpose, however general-purpose wire cutters can be used but might not cut the cable as neatly as the proper tool.

If fitting **Disc Brakes**, ensure you keep the rotors and pads clean during installation, avoid touching any of the braking surfaces. Take extra care to avoid spilling any lubrication or other fluids onto either the rotors or pads, especially when bleeding the brakes.

When fitting the calipers, you will need to centre the caliper to the rotor by applying the brakes whilst tightening – this may take a few attempts to eliminate any rubbing of the pads on the rotor.

It is advisable to bed-in new brakes after fitting by doing a series of heavy braking runs, you will typically notice that the braking performance improves as you go through this process.

Tuning the Bike to Fit

There are several parameters that allow you to adjust the **fit of the bike**; these are:

- For MTB: Suspension sag for forks and rear shock - which sets the initial stance of the bike;
- Saddle height;
- Saddle fore/aft position (sliding along the rails) and up-down rotation of the saddle;
- Handlebar height (via headset spacers and stem orientation);
- Handlebar rotation within the stem;
- Shifter position on the handlebars;
- Cleat position on shoe.

You can either set the above based on known measurements from other bikes or following YouTube instructions and using trial and error. However it is advisable (particularly for road bikes) to go for a professional **bike-fit**, whereby the above parameters will be adjusted to suit your body dimensions, flexibility and riding style.

In addition to the above, you may wish to include a bike-fit as part of the build process, whereby you could fit temporary handlebars (without bar tape), stem, saddle and seatpost and use the bike-fit to select the correct sizes for the final components. (Note: check with your bike-fitter for their guidelines on adopting this approach).

Bike as a Whole or Build Project?

You have now reached the end of the book and it is the time for the final decision whether you buy a whole bike or source individual components and build it yourself. The table below summarise the main considerations.

Benefits of Buying a Whole Bike	Benefits of DIY Build
Price – typically 20-30% cheaper if the spec is ok	You can specify every part to your exact needs
Guarantee if something breaks (but read the small-print)	Able to re-use any of your existing components
Potential change-of-mind policy if you don't like the bike (check with retailer on terms)	Satisfaction & education of building the bike yourself
Free initial service often included	Knowing how every part has been put together (rather than not knowing if parts have been lubricated or thread-locked etc.)
No need to assemble or buy tools	Knowledge and understanding such that you can maintain or repair the bike in the future.

Printed in Great Britain
by Amazon